The Witches' Almanac

Spring 2020—Spring 2021

CONTAINING pictorial and explicit delineations of the
magical phases of the Moon together with information about astrological
portents of the year to come and various aspects of occult knowledge
enabling all who read to improve their lives in the old manner.

The Witches' Almanac, Ltd.

Publishers   Providence, Rhode Island
www.TheWitchesAlmanac.com

Address all inquiries and information to
THE WITCHES' ALMANAC, LTD.
P.O. Box 1292
Newport, RI 02840-9998

13-ISBN: 978-1-881098-49-2

E-Book 13-ISBN: 978-1-881098-50-8

ISSN: 1522-3184

First Printing July 2019

Printed in USA

Established 1971 by Elizabeth Pepper

Preface

The summer seems to have come upon us very quickly this year. Changes in the seasons and local weather show a sign that many things are changing around us. We, at The Witches' Almanac, are changing too, by trying out something new this year. As a result of special customer needs (both shops and individual customers), The Witches' Almanac has released 2 editions of the Almanac: The Classic edition that you have come to know and love, and the Standard edition with a slight twist and which is marketed through Amazon and the chain bookstores. Only the Classic edition will be available through our website.

Although these two editions are very similar, a couple of changes have taken place. The Classic edition has remained priced at $12.95 and still contains the 15-month calendar that you have always seen.

The Standard edition is priced at $15.95 and contains a 12-month calendar. In addition, there is also an excerpt from one of our favorite author's newly released titles. This year, we have chosen Raven Grimassi's *What We Knew in the Night*.

The covers are slightly different as well, noting the edition type on the cover.

We only grow by changing. And, sometimes we need to change several times in order to grow into the best we can be. As The Witches' Almanac grows, we continue to adjust to our readership's wishes.

∽ HOLIDAYS ∾

Spring 2020 to Spring 2021

March 19	Vernal Equinox
April 1	All Fools' Day
April 30	Walpurgis Night
May 1	Beltane
May 7	Vesak Day
May 8	White Lotus Day
May 29	Oak Apple Day
June 5	Night of the Watchers
June 20	Summer Solstice
June 24	Midsummer
July 23	Ancient Egyptian New Year
July 31	Lughnassad Eve
August 1	Lammas
August 13	Diana's Day
August 17	Black Cat Appreciation Day
August 22	Ganesh Chaturthi
September 22	Autumnal Equinox
October 31	Samhain Eve
November 1	Hallowmas
November 16	Hecate Night
December 16	Fairy Queen Eve
December 17	Saturnalia
December 21	Winter Solstice
January 9	Feast of Janus
January 25	Chinese New Year
February 1	Oimelc Eve
February 2	Candlemas
February 15	Lupercalia
March 1	Matronalia
March 19	Minerva's Day

Art Director . . . . Gwion Vran

Astrologer . . . . Dikki-Jo Mullen

Climatologist . . . . Tom C. Lang

Cover Art and Design. . . . Kathryn Sky-Peck

Sales . . . . Ellen Lynch

Shipping, Bookkeeping . . . . . D. Lamoureux

ANDREW THEITIC
Executive Editor

JEAN MARIE WALSH
Associate Editor

ANTHONY TETH
Copy Editor

C O N T E N T S

C O N T E N T S

Ah Sun-flower! weary of time,

Who countest the steps of the Sun:

Seeking after that sweet golden clime

Where the travellers journey is done.

Where the Youth pined away with desire,
    And the pale Virgin shrouded in snow:

Arise from their graves and aspire,

Where my Sun-flower wishes to go.

Ah! Sun-flower, by William Blake
Ainsworth (1848)

Yesterday, Today and Tomorrow

by Timi Chasen

SPOTTED LEGIONS Meteorologists at the National Weather Service were briefly confounded by what appeared to be a massive raincloud formation, during what was meant to be an entirely clear day in Southern California. Seemingly out of nowhere, a sprawling cloud approximately ten miles wide appeared, and by the thickness of it on the doppler radar readouts, it looked much like a raincloud associated with a light to moderate precipitation. However, when they radioed to one of their spotters closer to the phenomena in question (Wrightwood, in San Bernadino County), they found not a cloud of moisture, but of ladybugs.

A ladybug 'bloom' is not an unnatural occurrence, having been known to happen occasionally during certain seasons when the conditions are just right for a huge population increase (say, shortly after a similar bloom of one of their favorite foods—aphids).

The diminutive spotted beetles are naturally keen to migrate, but the size and cohesion of the swarm has some scientists worried that it may be indicative of other problems, such as a sudden loss of sustainable habitat due to shifting weather patterns. For now, it will be chalked up as a bit of an anomaly, but Southwestern scientists will be keeping a close eye for any other signs of swarms on the move.

GHOSTLY WANDERINGS Narrow, meandering pathways through the countryside may have creepier histories than most realize. In old farming communities, particularly in the more isolated villages of England, corpse roads (also called coffin lines, lych ways or funeral roads) were specific paths used almost exclusively when dead bodies needed to be transferred to a proper burial ground outside of town. An interesting melding of superstitions very similar to those surrounding the corpse doors of Norse countries seem to have been at work here.

For a large portion of British history only the Church had the authority to deal with the dead (and accept them into consecrated ground). Since many isolated farming communities lacked a central parish, when someone perished there, their body would need to be transferred to a properly sanctified burying ground, else,

folklore reasoned, they would remain a cursed shade and wander the land, harassing those who crossed its path.

Corpse roads are specifically rambling and convoluted, with some reasoning they were to make certain the souls of the recently slain could not return and haunt their previous abodes, and it is said that the coffins were carried feet first so as to ensure the same. Since another superstition forbade the resting of the coffin upon the ground at any time during the transfer, specially chosen large stones were either installed or flattened along the morbid footpath in order to give the pallbearers places to temporarily rest their burden.

Since much superstition also surrounded the transfer of a dead body, the roads were abandoned for any other purpose, people fearing ill luck to those who wander the paths of the deceased.

ALL THAT BUZZ Super-sized yellow-jacket nests are becoming an increasing problem in the southern state of Alabama. Scientists are blaming the effects of climate change, which are causing warmer and warmer winter temperatures in the southern United States.

Typically, a series of cold fronts will kill off most of the wasps each year, as only the queen yellowjacket possesses the ability to hibernate overwinter (some have likened a chemical produced in her bloodstream to a natural antifreeze). However, if the temperature refrains from dropping low enough, almost all members of the hive will survive through the season (for, in some cases, multiple years in succession) and thrive unabated, eventually creating massive structures to house entirely new generations of wasps in addition to themselves.

Yellowjackets create their intricate nests by chewing pieces of woods and grinding them into a paste-like material that becomes a kind of paper when it dries. Some recently excavated super-hives (sometimes called perennial nests) found in Alabama and surrounding areas were said to be the size of large automobiles, with anywhere from twenty thousand to an incredible 250,000 insects (as found in a mammoth hive in South Carolina). Alabama scientists uncovered over ninety perennial nests in 2006, but that number may be quickly shattered in the upcoming years.

POSTHUMOUS JUSTICE The mayor of a picturesque Alpine town is calling for the reopening of a legal case over 300 years old. In the Northern Italian province of Trentino, a small town nestled within the mountain peaks named Brentonico is attempting to exonerate the memory of a woman tried, convicted, tortured and executed with some rather paltry evidence.

The magistrates of Alpine regions were notoriously cruel to those accused of Witchcraft, but now mayor Christian Perenzoni wishes to exonerate Maria Bertoletti Toldini, nicknamed "Toldina." In 1716 at the age of 60, Toldina was accused of practicing Witchcraft with the toxic gusto typical of the time period. Though her lawyer attempted to use reason with the judges, three young children had gone missing not long before the trial, and the rumor mill had surmised that Toldina was somehow responsible, even claiming she boiled a 5-year-old in a vat of cheese (without a shred of evidence, of course).

They sentenced her with a mélange of crimes that tended to be tacked onto most Witchcraft trials (sorcery, blasphemy, heresy, sodomy, etc.), and she was beheaded before her remains were burned. However, Perenzoni now wishes to reopen the case in a way that is legally binding, thus returning Toldina's ethical and civil dignity in a way recognized by the same court system that condemned her so many years ago.

We can only hope that more principalities stained with the blood of

innocents make such gestures of penance and good faith.

LOVE YOU TO DEATH Not far from Alabama in the State of Florida, different species of wasps are having far more trouble seeing their offspring survive. Though yellowjackets are highly social and live in hives, many other wasps are generally solitary, and make use of oak trees to feed their burgeoning young. An oak gall is a spherical home for a wasp larva created when an adult wasp uses a special proboscis to inject chemicals into parts of the tree which cause small, hard balls to form. The wasp then lays its egg into the gall and its young is both protected from predators and has meals provided for it as it slowly matures, eventually eating its way to freedom. However, there appears to be a new and unlikely predator making a dinner of these tiny insects.

The love vine (Cassytha filiformis) is a parasitic creeper plant native to most tropical regions, so-named due to its traditional use in aphrodisiacs and love potions. However, it appears to be a plant that purposefully seeks out and drains oak galls of their nutrients, thus starving the wasp larvae, who are usually unable to escape in time. In addition, they have been found to target the largest galls on a given tree.

Though scientists have been studying the disparate species independently for decades, they have only learned of this surprising behavior recently when they found multiple cases of oak galls entwined within vines of the plant, with many containing mummified wasp exoskeletons drained of their vitae.

Of 2000 regional galls examined, over 58% had been depleted by the love vine, which appears to be the first plant documented to attacks insect species in this manner. However, scientists believe they may be able to find far more in the near future, now that they know what to look for.

www.TheWitchesAlmanac.com

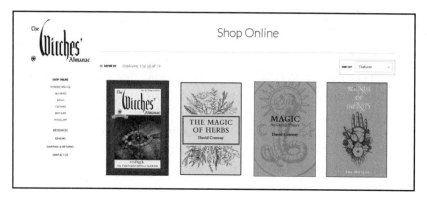

Come visit us at the Witches' Almanac website

News from The Witches' Almanac

Glad tidings from the staff

It has very much been a banner year at The Witches Almanac! As we put the finishing touches on this year's *Almanac*, we are also on press with another book and in the final phases of three more manuscripts. In all this busyness, we have kept a keen eye on needed improvements to our Web presence and optimizing our back office procedures.

We continue to receive positive feedback from you for TheWitchesAlmanac.com. We have responded by taking all the suggestions under consideration resulting in the streamlining of many of the ordering procedures. Of course, there are other areas of site worth checking on regularly such as *Author Bios*, *Seasonal Recipe* and *Sites of Awe*. Did you know that we run a special eight times a year, changing at each Sabbat. Go to TheWitchesAlmanac.com/shop-online/internet-special/ to view our latest internet special.

The Witches' Almanac is especially privileged to welcome new authors Sam Block, Phyllis Curott, Selena Fox, Lupa, Devin Hunter and Lord Alexian—each of whom have contributed incredible articles.

We are pleased to welcome Lee Morgan to our imprint. His latest tome, *Sounds of Infinity*, treats us to a comprehensive look at the world of Faery exploring geographical understanding, poetic understanding and finally presents a very workable grimoire. *Sounds of Infinity* can bought at TheWitchesAlmanac.com/SoundsofInfinity/.

David Conway has revised and updated his seminal work, *The Magic of Herbs*. Like many who were reared in a rural setting, David Conway came to know about healing arts that relied on a deep knowledge of herbal decoctions, tinctures and poultices. In this update of *The Magic of Herbs*, he shares the knowledge of herbs he gained in his early training in the hills of the Welsh countryside, as well as new emerging information. David studied with a master herbalist near his boyhood home, absorbing the practical and occult properties of the herbs and plants found in the surrounding environs.

It is with great pleasure that we announce that we are is now offering Atramentous Press' latest publication, *The Book of Q'ab iTz*. This tome appears as the vessel for the sorcerer, for contained within is the evidence of a practitioner who has dedicated the past few years to the arte magical. You can view Atramentous Press' publications at TheWitchesAlmanac.com/Atramentous/.

Stone Spelling

Delving Deeply into the Greek Alphabet Oracle

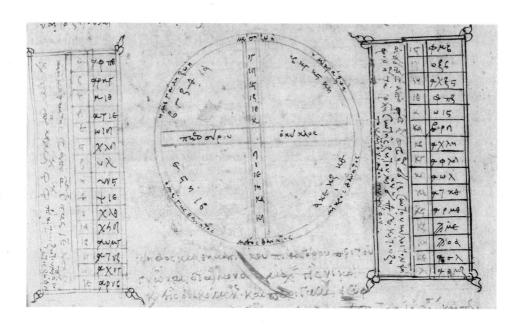

ANCIENT GREECE has been a well-spring of culture, inspiration and spirituality for so many of us, and in many cases Hellenic spiritual practices are a fine example of Leonardo da Vinci's saying that "simplicity is ultimate sophistication." I'm sure many of our endless varieties of cards and bones and sticks and stones that we use frequently in our work would dazzle an ancient Hellene, quickly followed by confusion: "Why so many different ways to do the same thing when but one would suffice? Use stones."

A common sight in ancient Greece was a pot full of stone tokens, used for anything from determining the verdict of a court to voting who should be exiled from the city. Even today, our word "ostracism" comes from the Greek *ostrakoi*, referring to broken shards of pottery recycled for use as tokens, but even these were a thrifty recycling of trash to replace what was likely originally *psēphoi*, little pebbles used as tokens for anything from counting to voting. In Aeschylus' tragedy *Eumenides*, Athena herself institutes the legal institution of trial by jury, where the jurors are to throw pebbles to tally up their votes. In some systems, they throw pebbles into different pots, in others, they throw pebbles of different colors, such as dark-colored stones for a guilty verdict and light-colored ones for not-guilty. Counting out the pebbles would yield a result to determine someone's fate; from this, the word *psēphos* took on a dual meaning, indicating both "pebble" as well as "judgment."

In Greece, drawing objects from a collection wasn't just used to determine the judgment of people on trial, but also to determine the judgment of fate itself. Sortilege is the proper term for any divination based on the random draw of lots, such as the pick of a card from a deck or drawing out a randomly-colored stone from a pot, and as a form of divination falls squarely under the purview of Hermes, the blessed messenger of the Gods. Yes, Apollon rules over prophecy, but he traded divination—which he felt was more childish than his own esteemed privilege to know the true mind of Zeus directly—to Hermes early on. In that light, any kind of tool-based method to divine the will of the Gods belongs to Hermes, who also coincidentally watches over all sorts of games of chance. Beyond that, Hermes is the God of communication, language, lore and all kinds of sciences and studies. What better method to divine to a Hellene with Hermes, than a combination of language and randomness?

Enter the system of *grammatomanteia*, or "divination by letters." In modern times called the "Greek Alphabet Oracle," after John Opsopaus who popularized it online back in the mid-1990s and more recently through his physical publications, this oracle has been known since at least the early 1900s when it was documented in archaeological finds in Hellenic sites in what is now modern Turkey. Based on

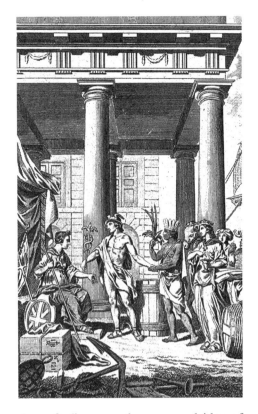

those findings, we have a good idea of how such an oracle worked.

Set up in a marketplace or other place accessible to the public would be a large pillar, inscribed with 24 different oracular verses, each verse beginning with a different letter of the Greek alphabet. By this pillar would be a pot of pebbles, each pebble also marked with a different letter. Say a prayer to Hermes or Apollon (the ancients considered them equivalent for this purpose), ask your question, draw out a stone from the pot and get your answer according to the verse on the pillar. Each verse from this vending machine-like oracle is a short one-line statement, like "All works will be successful, says the God" (Alpha, the best result the oracle can give) or "There is no fruit to take from a withered shoot" (Xi, meaning that you're barking up the wrong tree).

Let's say I wanted to know how to approach a new endeavor at work. I would go up to the oracle, raise my hands in supplication to the Gods and ask them what I wanted to know. Having done so, I'd reach into the pot and draw a letter, say, Gamma. Looking to the pillar, I'd read the associated oracle to be "The Earth will give you the ripe fruit of your labors" (*Gē soi teleion karpon apodōsei ponōn*). For me, this would indicate that everything would go amazing and my work would yield bountiful results, so long as I actually put in the effort needed to get them!

As far as divination methods go, it's simply elegant as much as elegantly simple, and could certainly be considered like a system of Greek "runes." Classically, however, this is about as far as it went; each letter had a simple verse associated with it, and that was that. Over the centuries since, however, the Greek letters have expanded their reach from one-line verses to encompass so much more—from the microcosmic to the macrocosmic, from parts of the body to the bodies of the Zodiac—and that's where this system can really shine. In the various methods of magic that have been developed in the West, there have been ways to develop a kind of "Greek kabbalah" of sorts, where the letters of the Greek alphabet can be delved into as a mystic system in their own right, letting Hermes guide us down endless paths of intrigue and mystery from simple stones.

Perhaps most valuable for us is the fact that the 24 letters in the Greek alphabet can be divided up into three groups, each associated with a different set of forces: the seven vowels (A, E, H, I, O, Y, Ω) for the seven traditional planets, the twelve simple consonants (B, Γ, Δ, Z, K, Λ, M, N, Π, P, Σ, T) for the twelve signs of the Zodiac, and the five complex consonants (Θ, Ξ, Φ, X, Ψ) for the five elements. Based on these associations, further correspondences to the Greek alphabet can be drawn, such as to words of power from the Greek Magical Papyri or to elder angels from the Coptic Magical Papyri, or to the different Gods and demigods of Mount Olympos and the rest of the Hellenic pantheon and cosmos.

Take the letter Lambda. In addition to having the verse "That which passes on the left bodes well for everything" (indicating that what appears to go badly will succeed in the end), this letter is also the sixth simple consonant, and so given to the sixth sign of the Zodiac, Virgo. Virgo is classically associated with the goddess of grain and growth, Demeter, the great matron of the Eleusinian Mysteries, and through her to the Horai, the deities of the seasons. Virgo (and thus Lambda) is also associated with Asteria, the Titan mother of Hekate, aunt to Apollon and Artemis, Goddess of falling stars and night- and star-based divination, which ties in nicely to the more Mercurial side of this sign of the Zodiac. On top of that, magical papyri give the word of power *Louloenēl* (*loo-loh-heh-nayl*), which can be used as a chant to focus all these powers together. Those of a more ceremonial or angelic bent might call on the forces of this letter through its angel, Labtiēl. Of course, we can't forget numerology either; Lambda has a value of 30, which reduces to 3 and ties it to that whole body of the wisdom of the numbers.

Nor can we forget the *Kyranides*, either! This venerable proto-grimoire has been famous throughout the Western world since the 4th century, cataloging all sorts of stones, animals and plants, and all kinds of magical and medical works that could be done with them, all categorized by their Greek names in a kind of alphabetical index for the cosmos. Turning to the *Kyranides* for Lambda, for instance, one can find that this letter is also tied to the wolf (*lykos*), hare (*lagōos*), seagull (*laros*), vulture (*lynx*), glow-worm (*lampouris*), bass fish (*labrax*), frankincense (*libanon*) and the stone lingurius or *lyncurium*, a kind of yellow amber-colored stone now thought to be a kind of jacinth or tourmaline. Endless recipes, concoctions and applications are given for all sorts of reasons, such as curing illnesses of the eyes, ensuring victory in all causes, casting out phantasms, healing shivering fevers and other such miracles. All this falls under the letter Lambda, all tied together in a letter-microcosm of its own.

All this within a single cast of a single pebble. With twenty-four such pebbles, containing whole worlds unto themselves, Hermes surely has plenty to keep us busy with his games! All we need to do is ask for but a moment of guidance and off we go, all with picking out a single stone.

It must be remembered that Greeks maintained a powerful connection between letters and numbers: what we call *gematria*, they called *isopsēphia*, originally referring to an equality of votes (see the word *psēphos* hidden in there?), but which was used to denote tallying up the numerical value of letters which, for them, did double duty as numbers. Throughout the centuries, this ancient Hellenic connection between letters, numbers, divination and judgment has been with us all along with little pebbles that served them in countless tasks to communicate from on high to down low, whether in courts of law or courts of the Gods. We can tap into that ancient tradition, too, with just a handful of stones at our side. Perhaps by this, we too can learn the mystery of the letter Psi: *Psēphon dikaian ēnde para theōn echeis*, "You have this righteous judgment-stone from the Gods."

—SAM BLOCK

Railroad Spikes & Magic

MADE OF IRON, forged in flame, driven through the ground and used to tie tracks together, the railroad spike is perhaps one of the most powerful tools we can work with today in modern Witchcraft. What makes their usage in magic particularly interesting is that the practice is relatively new as we know it, likely coming from African American and Chinese American cultures at the turn of the 20th century, and later becoming popularized with the rise of magical folk traditions in the United States. Because they are made from iron, we often think of them as articles of protection, but their potential uses extend beyond that, if you can get your hands on the right kind of railroad spike.

It is common these days to find baskets full of shiny new railroad spikes at your local metaphysical and occult shop, and while it can be tempting to grab them for your workings, you might want to think twice. The most prized and powerful spikes have been used to tie tracks together and keep a train on course. In our magic we aren't just harnessing the power of the iron it is made of, we are harnessing its history. One that should no doubt be full of wear and tear. It is often said the best way to come across one is to go for a walk along a railroad. There you will find spikes that have been naturally discarded and those are the ones you want for your workings. It is, of course, not recommended that you pry spikes from tracks as that could cause a serious accident.

The most common working involves nailing one spike into each corner of a property for protection. The origin of this working comes from a spell to keep the bank or other lenders from taking your home. Protection, yes, but not in the way we usually think of it. To seal the spell, you would place a silver dime on the head of each nail along with some graveyard dirt before burying it, and of course, urinating on it to mark it as your own. More recent variations of this working modify it to focus on more physical and spiritual concerns, excluding the silver dollar, graveyard dirt and urine altogether.

Along the same lines, we can work with them to help tie something or someone down—say a lover who likes to stray or even cattle that might escape. To do this, take a piece of parchment or brown bag and write the name of the person or thing that you want to tie down three times. Rotate the paper 90° clockwise and write the words "STAY WITH ME" three times over the column of names. Once you have done this, use your pen to write "You cannot leave, you will not stray, you are bound to me!" three times in a circle around the crossed names at the center. Wrap this petition paper around a railroad spike and then fix it by tightly wrapping a red cord or ribbon around the spike. Under a dark Moon hammer the spike into the ground, or if needed, place it under the altar.

An oil can be made using an old railroad spike which can be used not only for protection and to assist in the tying down of things, but to increase stamina and break curses as well! To make the oil place a used railroad spike in a jar and fill it with carrier oil (such as sweet almond, fractionated coconut, or even olive) until it covers the top of the spike by about one inch. Place this in a dark and cool place for three months to charge. After three months, the oil will be ready for use and you should remove the spike from the glass jar before mixing in any other oils or ingredients that you might want to add, helping to avoid glass breaks. You can, however, leave the spike in the oil to continue charging for as long as the shelf-life of the oil. To one half-oz of this oil, blend in three drops rue essential oil and seven drops hyssop essential oil to create a hex-breaking condition oil. Follow

the same process but instead of rue and hyssop oils, add nine drops frankincense and five drops calendula to increase physical stamina. You can also apply the oil on its own as an aide in any protection working without the need of additional essential oils.

Lastly, railroad spikes can be used to increase stability in just about any area of our lives. Think of any aspect of your life that could use some stability and boil it down to one word, or a sigil for those who work with them. Put that word or sigil on all four sides of a railroad spike using either chalk or paint. On the top of the spike, draw a pentacle with the same chalk or paint. Drive this spike into the ground in front of your front door (a flower pot on the inside of your apartment entrance will do nicely, too!) to attract stability in that area of your life.

Railroad spikes can be worked into just about any spell that requires strength, durability, or stamina, and let's face it—there aren't too many workings that can't benefit from those each of things. Just be sure to grab one with a history.

—DEVIN HUNTER

GODDESS OF NO ESCAPE

ON A LONELY STRETCH of Attica coastline, a mere 40 miles northeast of Athens, is the ruined temple of the long-forgotten Goddess whose cult would surely merit revival today. Originally a rural deity, worshiped as a local variation of the huntress Artemis, she became widely known as Nemesis, Goddess of just retribution and persecutor of the excessively rich and proud. She was sometimes called Adrasteria, meaning "one from whom there is no escape."

Patroness of gladiators, worshiped in Rome by victorious generals, Nemesis was known to everyone in ancient times for taking particular care of the presumptuous and especially punishing hubris—the unpardonable crime of considering oneself master of one's own destiny.

But Nemesis of Rhamnous was how she was known; and the once-flourishing Rhamnous, a busy fortress town protecting the grain cargoes shipped across the narrow straits of Euboea, is now as abandoned and deserted as a Goddess herself. Overgrown by the prickly scrub that gave the place its name, it is unreachable save by car or on foot, visited by less than one in 10,000 tourists, and accessible by bus only as far as Grammatiko or Ayia marina, both several miles away.

Rhamnous' best-known native son was the orator Antiphon (c. 480 BCE) whose school of rhetoric included Thucydides among its illustrious pupils. Built in 436 BCE by the same (unknown) architect responsible for the Poseidon temple at Cape Sounion and the temples to Hephaistos and Ares in Athens' Roman Agora, the Nemesis temple adjoined an earlier—and smaller—one on the site shared by a similar Goddess, Themis. Her special responsibilities were law, equity, and custom. Thus the Goddesses of "Just Order" and "Righteous Vengeance" would seem to be a harmonious match.

Originally measuring about 35 feet by 66 feet with twelve columns, fluted top and bottom, with gilded cornices bearing lotus decorations and lions' heads along the roof gutters through which rain escaped, the Doric temple was constructed from nearby marble whose workings still bear ancient tool marks. Sometime between being rededicated to Augustus' late wife Livia who died in 29 CE, and its excavation in 1813, the temple was ravaged and remained that way. It was the custom of the Greeks to leave in their ruined state and not restore temples that had been destroyed by "barbarians."

Nobody knows what Nemesis really looked like. Fragments of a large head discovered in the ruins (and now in the British Museum) were said to have been part of a statue of Aphrodite entered in a contest and renamed when not chosen, later to be sold by the sculptor, Agorakritos of Paros on condition it not be exhibited in Athens. Pausanias, writing about all this 600 years later, said that the actual sculptor was Agorakritos' famous teacher,

Phidias, and that the Nemesis statue was carved out of a block of marble brought a cross by the Persians in 490 BCE and intended for a "victory" statue when they had won the battle of Marathon in the nearby marshes. The Persians, of course, lost that one and as an example of hubris this story of the statue's origin is perhaps too good to be true.

Certainly was true that Nemesis was being worshiped locally well before that celebrated battle and even before the temple was built. It was the custom in those days for a year's garrison duty outside Athens to be served by all youths of military age; and at Rhamnous the recruits participated in torch races in honor of the Goddess, while in Athens itself an annual Nemesian festival was held.

Herodotus, born a half-dozen years after the Greeks' glorious victory at Marathon, made much of the Nemesis cult, as can be seen by his writings which refer constantly to the theme of some power that brought retribution. And, of course, the Goddess has the usual colorful history common to her kind. Pursued by Zeus but unwilling to mate with him, she kept changing her shape until, caught while she was disguised as a goose, she gave birth to a hyacinth-colored egg which, under the guidance of Leda, was hatched as Helen: that same Helen over which the Trojan war was subsequently fought.

At the base of the statue found in the temple of Nemesis, this tale of her encounter with Zeus was told in relief sculpture. Seen (and described) by Pausanias in its entirety, it remains today only as disconnected fragments.

BRIDGING THE WORLDS WITH MUSIC

MUSIC IS A BRIDGE between the world of humanity and the Gods. It is a tool that is often forgotten within private ritual and personal practices. When you are within a group of people, it is easier to sing and chant along with others. But when you are alone, it often feels silly to sing, drum and chant when no one is listening. The truth is, YOU are listening and so are the Gods.

Experiment with music, drumming and chanting. Through experimentation you may stumble upon the amazing experience of entrainment, a magickal occurrence unto itself. Entrainment is the bio-musicological synchronization of an organism to an externally perceived rhythm. This happens when African drummers drum together, or when anyone taps their foot with others in the audience to the same rhythm. However, it is not simply staying together "on the beat," but rather a deeper understanding of connectedness that can only be experienced.

The five senses of the human experience can be attributed to the elements and sound encompasses them all.

Hearing

Spirit or Ether is related to hearing; it is the source, the all. From silence comes sound, which returns to silence. We know the beginning and we know the end, the Alpha and the Omega. This can be looked at in different ways, including quantum theory. Cymatics uses sound waves to rearrange simple matter like sand, oil, water or clay into geometrical patterns, known as Chalinadi Figures. These figures resemble the same patterns illustrated as the underlying quantum field in quantum mechanics; the way the universe is constantly being created by the union of pulsing energy on the quantum field. As above, so below.

Touch

Next comes Air, which can be heard and felt. You cannot see air, only the effects of it. You do not smell or taste the air, only what the air carries within it, including electrical charges.

Sight

Fire can be heard, felt and seen. Whether you realize it or not, you cannot smell fire, only the smoke, which is being created from what fire is consuming. Of course, you cannot taste fire.

Taste

Water can be heard, felt, seen and tasted.

Smell

Earth can be heard, felt, seen, tasted and smelled.

In this pattern, it immediately becomes interesting to the Wiccan that the senses of Earth and Air are flipped. In Wicca, the element of Air is usually attributed to the sense of smell, and the element of Earth is usually attributed to the sense of touch. It's worth consideration to spend some time contemplating this alternate pattern.

The path from this realm to spirit begins with the magickal motto of the earth Element: to keep silent. That is why the Pagan religions and practices work so well. They work from without (utilizing the cycles of seasons, lunar phases, and physical tools and correspondences) to within (illuminating the shadows and purging what is unneeded mentally and spiritually) and back out again. To ground spirit into our lives, we must learn to LISTEN, for sound is the gateway to spirit.

Sometimes spiritual experiences are described in terms of "vibes" or vibrations. It is interesting to note that all vibrations are related and can be placed upon one graphic scale measured in frequencies and wavelengths. In sound, wavelengths can be larger than skyscrapers (subsonic). When looking at the electromagnetic spectrum they can be as small as the width of a subatomic particle (cosmic gamma rays). Some waves can penetrate our atmosphere, some cannot. Also, some sound waves can penetrate earth/houses, some cannot. It depends on the length of the wave and what it is trying to penetrate.

With frequency, the faster the vibration, the higher the pitch and type of wave. We start low and slow with subsonic sound, then comes audible sound. Humans can only hear part of this spectrum, if they have perfect hearing, from around 20 Hz to 20,000 Hz. If you purchase a pair of expensive headphones that go above 20kHz, only your dog will be able to hear it. Next is AM radio, followed by shortwave radio, television, FM radio, radar, until we hit such a frequency pitch that we get to the light. First infrared light that allows us to see in the dark, then visible light, followed by ultraviolet light. Finally, we get x-rays, gamma rays and other higher cosmic rays.

As you can see, it is one thing. Vibrations are vibrations, it is the speed with which they come toward you that makes the difference. There are probably many more types of energetic vibrations out there that our current instruments do not yet detect.

Mentioned earlier is experimentation with sound, rhythm and music. Below is an example of the twelve classical Greek/Roman Gods as they could relate to the 12-tone western scale. A musical interval is the distance between two notes. This list is based on the "feeling"

that intervals from music theory lend to chords, it is not necessarily mathematical or logical. In fact, in ancient Greece, the minor pentatonic scale (a five-note scale) was used along with others. It was Pythagoras, a Greek Philosopher, that is attributed to DIS-covering our modern western musical scale by using mathematical ratios.

Let's dive into this musical thought experiment:

C—Zeus/Jupiter, King of the Gods

Ancient Greece and Rome were patriarchal societies and at the base, the beginning, is the King of the Gods, Zeus. Therefore, he gets attributed to the musical letter C. When examining C in music theory and chord scales, the root of the chord is the foundation, the father of all

other tones to follow; the root of the musical scale.

C#/Db—Hera/Juno, Queen of the Gods

The second one, the sister, the Goddess of birth, but also vengeful and jealous of the others that followed. In music theory C#/Db when coupled with C forms a minor 2nd. It rubs. It is dissonant, but at the same time, there is movement and growth. It also does not necessarily play well with all the notes that follow, but it does sound nice with A#/Bb (Ares/Mars).

D—Poseidon/Neptune, God of the Sea

It is "Re" in solfege, always present, a layer which covers, moving the ear either up or down depending on how you approach it. Less dissonant than C#/Db, when D is played with C it forms a major 2nd which is still dissonant and moody, like Poseidon. It is stated that the key of D minor is the saddest key to write a song in, as it affects the listener so strongly, causing waves of emotion.

D#/Eb—Hephaestus/Vulcan, God of the Forge and Fire

Hard working and responsible, D#/Eb coupled with C creates a minor 3rd. It is highly useful in music and creates many powerful melodies and harmonies. Minor keys are most often used for sad songs, but also for dance music, which has a beat or rhythm of the anvil.

E—Aphrodite/Venus, Goddess of Love and Beauty

The Goddess of Beauty is attributed here to the note E. When people try and "harmonize" the first interval that humans go for is a major 3rd.

That is what C and E form in music theory. It makes the melody sound "pretty." It makes harmonies "major" or sound "happy."

F—Artemis/Diana, Goddess of Wild Things, Huntress

When F is coupled with C, you get a major 4th. This interval is hard to hear in the major scale; it is also one of the most unique. It is used in all subdominant and dominant chords in a major key. It brings unrest and forward movement in a harmonic progression. The Huntress is running through the wood, wild and untamed, yet providing and protecting her own. When mixed with the pentatonic scale, the interval of the 4th gives way to the unique sound of older Asian music.

F#/Gb—Athena/Minerva, Goddess of Wisdom and War

This interval of a tritone between C and F#/Gb is the most unstable of sounds in the 12-tone scale and the hardest to hear and sing. It sounds like a train whistle or battle horn, announcing to all within range to beware! The tritone interval divides the octave perfectly in half, laying down the line of demarcation that one dares not cross in battle.

G—Apollo/Helios, God of Music

The interval between C and G is called a perfect 5th in music theory. It resonates so strongly it is found in most chords, except diminished and augmented chords. The perfect 5th is the basis of the guitar "power chord" found in most heavy metal and rock music. The absence of the 3rd (E) in a "power chord" makes a shimmering, open, vitalizing sound. The perfect 5th describes Apollo, the God of Music, ever-present, the Sun, the light, and healing. Triumphant Tiphareth for all to see.

G#/Ab—Hermes/Mercury, God of Travelers, the Eloquent Messenger, storyteller, prone to cliffhangers, keeper of the gate, a traveler between the worlds.

Found in augmented chords, the G#/Ab tone coupled with C brings an augmented 5th. Commonly called a "sting chord," an augmented 5th chord in its full four note form is what you hear in cheesy soap-operas when shock and dismay, underscoring as if to say "No! It cannot be!" The God Hermes/Mercury, the messenger, often shocked the recipients of his news.

A—Eros/Cupid, God of Love

Between C and A lies the interval of a major 6th. Next, to the major 3rd and perfect 5th, this is the 3rd most common pitch that is utilized when trying to harmonize. Usually, it draws the ear into a sad minor key, which is of course how Cupid's quiver usually finds its next victim—in the throes of love pain, before, during and after. It is worth noting that the perfect 5th up from A is E, Aphrodite.

A#/Bb—Ares/Mars, God of War

At A#/Bb we arrive at Ares, God of War. The Bb with a C produces the interval of a minor 7th. It is present in dominant chords, chords that MUST advance and resolve. There is strife in a dominant chord, and something must move to resolve it—war. The E (Aphrodite) in the dominant chord gives way to Eb (Vulcan), and we have sadness in the minor 7th chord. The sadness of war. Hephaestus forges swords and weapons of war. Whether

marching to conquer or to contemplate the tools of war, Bb belongs to Ares.

B—Hades/Pluto, God of the Underworld

You may be asking why the top note would be associated with the God of the Underworld. Well, in music, octaves repeat. So, we start over with C again. So really B is at once a minor 2nd below C as much as it is a major 7th above C. Both are highly dissonant. However, when you mix in E (Aphrodite) and G (Apollo), a major 7th chord blooms into existence showing us how death and life are combined and support each other in one beautiful arrangement of cosmic harmony.

No matter how you approach it, sound and music touch us deep inside in ways no other magickal instruments of influence can. Learn to listen.

—ALEXIAN

Lord Alexian's site can be found at https://alexianmusic.com/

Intention, Attention, and Story-Telling

Notes Toward a General Theory of Magic, Part IV

A THOUSAND YEARS AGO, in the newly christianized northern German lands, some Christian priest wrote down two magic spells on a blank page of a manuscript. We now call them the *Merseburg spells*, after the city where the manuscript has been kept for centuries. Although the manuscript is mostly in Latin, the priest wrote down those two spells in his every-day spoken language (an ancient form of German).

The Merseburg spells are among the very oldest magic spells that have come down to us from the Middle Ages anywhere in Europe. Not only are they very old, but they are also explicitly Pagan. They mention Woden (Odin) and other powerful Beings from ancient Germanic myth and lore. There is not the least hint of Christianity in them.

The two Merseburg spells were meant to free the limbs of a person or animal from every sort of constraint. The first spell frees them from every bond and fetter, either mundane or magical. The second heals every physical injury to a limb, such as a sprain or a bruise or a break. One insightful scholar conjectured that the priest who copied them into his book had himself become painfully lame, and had resolved to make use of Pagan spells as well as Christian prayers if that was what it took to heal his legs.

It is the second of the two Merseburg spells that interests us here. It may be translated as follows, keeping the word order and every ambiguity of the original:

> Phol and Woden rode to the wood
> There Balder's foal wrenched
>   his foot.
> Then bespelled it Sinthgut,
>   Sunna her sister,
> Then bespelled it Friia, Folla
>   her sister,
> Then bespelled it Woden, as he
>   well knew how.
> As bone-wrench, as blood-wrench,
>   as limb-wrench:
> Bone to bone, blood to blood,
>   limb to limbs,
> So they are joined!

This spell exemplifies many things that we have already discussed in the first three of these Notes. It is, first of all, **performative** speech. It employs three-fold parallel constructions **(patterns and the law of contiguity)**. It names powerful Deities and Beings (symbols and the law of similarity). It has a fairly high **coefficient of weirdness**.

No one now knows who Phol was, or Sinthgut. We can only guess at the identities of Sunna (Sun?), Friia (Freyja?) and Folla (Full Moon?). We are not even quite sure that Balder is the name of a God, not a title meaning "Lord." Even a thousand years ago, when the spell was first composed, it may have been only a rare expert in the myth and magic of his people who knew the full tales of those Beings.

The Three Parts of a Traditional European Folk Spell

The first five lines of the Merseburg spell tell a little story, a **historiola**,

about the Pagan God Woden and some companions. (*Historiola* just means a "little story" in Latin.) Very many old traditional folk spells begin with a *historiola* that calls to mind some past act of a powerful Being that is meant to be done again when the spell is uttered.

The next two lines state the spell's purpose and command its fulfillment; they are called the spell's **intent**. Whether it is a bone or a blood-vessel or a limb that has been injured ("wrenched"), the spell restores it to wholeness: *Bone to bone, blood to blood, limb to limbs*.

The final line is the spell's **ratification**, that is, a form of words announcing that the work of the spell has now been accomplished: *So they are joined!*

These are the three parts of many a traditional spell in Europe: **historiola, intent, and ratification**.

Several hundred years later, variants of the second Merseburg spell have been recorded. They come from almost every country of northern Europe, and every century from the

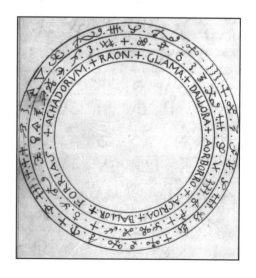

1300s down to the 1900s. Every one of these later variants has a less elaborate historiola than the Merseburg spell, or no *historiola* at all. When there is a historiola, it is Jesus or some Christian saint who rides and who heals the mount's injured leg.

Ceremonial Animals—Talking Animals—Story-Telling Animals

So *why* do so many traditional folk spells begin with a *historiola*? Is it more than just a matter of convention and habit? The answer to that question lies in human nature, in the ways in which our biology predisposes us to act.

We humans are **talking animals**. We talk to pass on information. We talk to get things done. We talk to figure things out. And quite often we talk—without paying attention to the meaning of our words—simply in order to strengthen the ties that bind us together into communities. By this kind of talking we **commune** with one another, even though we are not **communicating** anything in particular to our fellows. This last sort of talking, mere social chatter, Bronislaw Malinowski called **phatic communion**. (*Phatic* means "talking," so phatic communion means communion achieved by talking.)

We humans are also **ceremonial animals**, as the philosopher Ludwig Wittgenstein once noted while reading Frazer's *The Golden Bough*. We have a strong biological instinct to perform ceremonies and rituals, whether as part of a group or alone. We do this for much the same reasons that we talk: rituals pass on information, rituals get things done, rituals help

us figure things out. Shared rituals establish *communion* among people, just like shared speech. Like speech, too, rituals can be a means of gaining power over our lives and our world. And finally, humans have a natural hunger for the sacred. Rituals are able to satisfy that hunger. They can strengthen the presence of the sacred in our lives. Whether simple or complex, short or long, rituals are everywhere in human life.

And finally, we humans are **story-telling animals**. We weave stories into almost every conversation. Quite often these stories are very simple ones, so short that we do not think of them as stories at all. Yet, for example, when we explain to our boss why we failed to complete some required task, what is our tale of excuses but a very simple story about ourselves and our situation?

Often, too, we tell stories of much greater import than that example, and

we tell them in far more detail, with far greater artistry. Such stories, when we tell them about ourselves, can even help us *define*—nay, *create*!—our very identities as individual human beings, either in our own right or as members of some community. By such stories we map out the courses of our own lives from birth to death, and in the process we also give our lives meaning.

The most powerful of these stories can even suggest solutions to the hardest problems of our human lives, or give answers to the deepest riddles of our existence. Stories of this kind are the great **myths**, which (as the Neo-Platonist philosopher Sallustius wisely said) tell of "things that never happened, but always are."

And it must be noted, stories of such power as these can also inspire their tellers to create new rituals and ceremonies, in which these myths are enshrined for all time to come. **Myth** and **ritual** evolve together over the centuries as two parts of the same whole, two sides of the same coin. There is an eternal synergy between them.

The Story-Teller's Paradox

But herein also lies a paradox. We commonly say that *we tell our stories.* Is it perhaps more true to say that *our stories tell us*? Which comes first, the person or the story?

People do indeed shape the stories they tell. Yet the more powerful a story is, the more it *also* shapes the people who tell it and who hear it told. Powerful stories, too, outlive the people who tell them, as well as those who have told them. The great myths have been passed down from one generation to the next through all the long ages of history, and will continue to be passed on as long as there are humans to tell and hear them.

The poet Muriel Rukeyser once wrote, with very deep insight, "The universe is made of stories, not of atoms."

She was speaking, of course, about the universe that we humans experience, about the world in which we live and move and have our being—**not** about that other, quite alien universe studied by the physical sciences, that vast impersonal unstoried world of matter and energy that spans all time and all space, that is fettered and shaped by the iron laws of cause and effect. These two universes are two quite different things. No magician worth his salt can ever afford to forget that truth.

We have no *unmediated* knowledge of the second of these universes, that alien world of matter and energy, time and space, cause and effect. Everything that we do know of it is *mediated*, that is, it gets inside our skins only by passing through the mighty filters of our sense organs and our nervous and endocrine systems. Once it has passed through those filters, it is memory and thought alone shaping it into words, images and patterns that we can then use as we live out our lives. This is *how* we are able to tell stories at all, and also *why* we tell them. And as we tell these stories, they shape us and we shape them. Here again there is eternal synergy.

This is why the universe in which our human consciousness moves and lives and has its being is indeed *made of stories, not of atoms*. This is the story-teller's paradox. This, too, is why magicians and story-tellers are close kin to one another.

Attention and Intention

Be all this as it may, there are few things that can rivet a person's attention as strongly as a well-told story of great power. If the story goes hand-in-hand with a well-crafted ritual, then attention is riveted even more strongly. (In part, this is why rituals of initiation and rites of passage are essential to the long-term well-being of every society, including our own. But that is best left for another article.)

It is commonplace among magicians that any work of magic can be effective only if the magicians begin their work with a clear, well-defined **intention**, and if they hold that intention firmly in mind while they see their work through to completion. If they don't, they are thought to have worked in vain.

However, this commonplace is not quite true. A traditional folk spell or ritual may have had a quite precise intention built into its very structure by the magicians who first created it, or who passed it down from one generation to the next, changing its words and actions slightly to meet the new demands of changed times. The second Merseburg spell is such a spell, as is each of its later variants. Its **intention** is built into its words and its actions, from its *historiola* through its intent to its ratification. (A spell's intention it is over-all purpose and aim, whereas a traditional folk spell's intent is the second of its three parts. *Intention* and *intent* are related, but they are not at all the same thing.)

Later magicians who use that spell can take intention for granted, so long as they work the spell or ritual in its traditional way. (This is true not only of magical rituals, but of any traditional ritual, including religious, civic and social ones.) Such rituals draw their power *ex opere operato*,

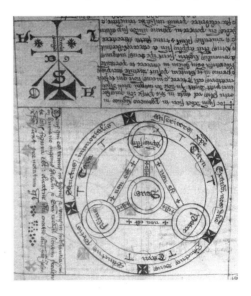

"from the work that has been worked," much more than from the people who work them.

In addition to a magician's **intention**, there is also the **attention** that magicians pay to each work of magic as they work it. Distraction is an ancient enemy of effective magic. One challenge that every magician must face is how to rivet attention on the work of magic that is being performed, for it is attention that enhances the power of a spell.

In a traditional folk spell, it is the *historiola* at its beginning that captures attention. As already noted, there are few things that can hold a person's attention as fully as a well-told story of great power. Yet if the story is too elaborate, it will distract attention from the magic itself. This is why a traditional folk spell often begins with a *historiola* that alludes to some traditional myth, but does not retell it fully. The *historiola* must be long enough to call the myth to mind, but not so long as to distract people from the spell's *intent* and *ratification*.

It is no easy thing to *pay attention*, and it is almost as hard to grasp what paying attention involves in a person's real life. Perhaps an example may help make it clear.

In a big city on the Atlantic coast there lives an elderly magician who writes under the pen-name of Draja Mickaharic. He has been giving lessons in magic for half a century now. One of his last students has published an instructive account of the early lessons in magic that he learned from Draja (Luke Cullen, *Growing Up With Draja Mickaharic*, 2009). Luke tells how his very first lesson with Draja, back around 1987, began when Draja said to him, "I want you to pay attention." At first Luke supposed that a full lesson would follow those words, but he soon was told that "Pay attention!" actually was the entire first lesson. Draja explained that he had just assigned Luke the very difficult task of learning to pay attention to *everything* in his life: to his own posture, to the rhythm of his breathing, to the smell and feel of the air around him, to the quality of the light or darkness in each moment, to all the other people around him, to what they are doing, to the expressions on their faces, and so forth. He was to practice paying attention to all these things and to everything around him for a whole year. After a year of doing this, Luke could come back to Draja for his second lesson.

I do not know of any other story that shows so clearly how important it is in magic to develop the habit of constantly paying attention to everything, and just how very hard it is to master that skill. (It is also a very useful skill to develop for one's mundane life, too.)

Looking Forward

With this we end the fourth of these *Notes Toward a General Theory of Magic*. The fifth of these Notes will appear in the next issue of *The Witches' Almanac*. It will deal with the role of the human body in magic, and with poppets. There will be at least one further Note, the sixth. It will discuss the differences between the physical world, the imaginal world, and imaginary worlds, and the significance of the imaginal world for magic.

—ROBERT MATHIESEN

Hans Christian Andersen

The Darning-Needle

THERE WAS ONCE a darning-needle who thought herself so fine that she fancied she must be fit for embroidery. "Hold me tight," she would say to the fingers, when they took her up, "don't let me fall; if you do I shall never be found again, I am so very fine."

"That is your opinion, is it?" said the fingers, as they seized her round the body.

"See, I am coming with a train," said the darning-needle, drawing a long thread after her; but there was no knot in the thread.

The fingers then placed the point of the needle against the cook's slipper. There was a crack in the upper leather, which had to be sewn together.

"What coarse work!" said the darning-needle, "I shall never get through. I shall break!—I am breaking!" and sure enough she broke. "Did I not say so?" said the darning-needle, "I know I am too fine for such work as that."

"This needle is quite useless for sewing now," said the fingers; but they still held it fast, and the cook dropped some sealing-wax on the needle, and fastened her handkerchief with it in front.

"So now I am a breast-pin," said the darning-needle; "I knew very well I should come to honor some day: merit is sure to rise;" and she laughed, quietly to herself, for of course no one ever saw a darning-needle laugh. And there she sat as proudly as if she were in a state coach, and looked all around her. "May I be allowed to ask if you are made of gold?" she inquired of her neighbor, a pin; "you have a very pretty appearance, and a curious head, although you are rather small. You must take pains to grow,

for it is not every one who has sealing-wax dropped upon him;" and as she spoke, the darning-needle drew herself up so proudly that she fell out of the handkerchief right into the sink, which the cook was cleaning. "Now I am going on a journey," said the needle, as she floated away with the dirty water, "I do hope I shall not be lost." But she really was lost in a gutter. "I am too fine for this world," said the darning-needle, as she lay in the gutter; "but I know who I am, and that is always some comfort." So the darning-needle kept up her proud behavior, and did not lose her good humor. Then there floated over her all sorts of things,—chips and straws, and pieces of old newspaper. "See how they sail," said the darning-needle; "they do not know what is under them. I am here, and here I shall stick. See, there goes a chip, thinking of nothing in the world but himself—only a chip. There's a straw going by now; how he turns and twists about! Don't be thinking too much of yourself, or you may chance to run against a stone. There swims a piece of newspaper; what is written upon it has been forgotten long ago, and yet it gives itself airs. I sit here patiently and quietly. I know who I am, so I shall not move."

One day something lying close to the darning-needle glittered so splendidly that she thought it was a diamond; yet it was only a piece of broken bottle. The darning-needle spoke to it, because it sparkled, and represented herself as a breast-pin. "I suppose you are really a diamond?" she said.

"Why yes, something of the kind," he replied; and so each believed the other to be very valuable, and then they began to talk about the world, and the conceited people in it.

"I have been in a lady's work-box," said the darning-needle, "and this lady was the cook. She had on each hand five fingers, and anything so conceited as these five fingers I have never seen; and yet they were only employed to take me out of the box and to put me back again."

"Were they not high-born?"

"High-born!" said the darning-needle, "no indeed, but so haughty. They were five brothers, all born fingers; they kept very proudly together, though they were of different lengths. The one who stood first in the rank was named the thumb, he was short and thick, and had only one joint in his back, and could therefore make but one bow; but he said that if he were cut off from a man's hand, that man would be unfit for a soldier. Sweet-tooth, his neighbor, dipped himself into sweet or sour, pointed to the sun and moon, and formed the letters when the fingers wrote. Longman, the middle finger, looked over the heads of all the others. Gold-band, the next finger, wore a golden circle round his waist. And little Playman did nothing at all, and seemed proud of it. They were boasters, and boasters they will remain; and therefore I left them."

"And now we sit here and glitter," said the piece of broken bottle.

At the same moment more water streamed into the gutter, so that it overflowed, and the piece of bottle was carried away.

"So he is promoted," said the darning-needle, "while I remain here; I am too fine, but that is my pride, and what do I care?" And so she sat there in her pride, and had many such thoughts as these,— "I could almost fancy that I came from a sunbeam, I am so fine. It seems as if the sunbeams were always looking for me under the water. Ah! I am so fine that even my mother cannot find me. Had I still my old eye, which was broken off, I believe I should weep; but no, I would not do that, it is not genteel to cry."

One day a couple of street boys were paddling in the gutter, for they sometimes found old nails, farthings, and other treasures. It was dirty work, but they took great pleasure in it. "Hallo!" cried one, as he pricked himself with the darning-needle, "here's a fellow for you."

"I am not a fellow, I am a young lady," said the darning-needle; but no one heard her.

The sealing-wax had come off, and she was quite black; but black makes a person look slender, so she thought herself even finer than before.

"Here comes an egg-shell sailing along," said one of the boys; so they stuck the darning-needle into the egg-shell.

"White walls, and I am black myself," said the darning-needle, "that looks well; now I can be seen, but I hope I shall not be sea-sick, or I shall break again." She was not sea-sick, and she did not break. "It is a good thing against sea-sickness to have a steel stomach, and not to forget one's own importance. Now my sea-sickness has past: delicate people can bear a great deal."

Crack went the egg-shell, as a waggon passed over it. "Good heavens, how it crushes!" said the darning-needle. "I shall be sick now. I am breaking!" but she did not break, though the waggon went over her as she lay at full length; and there let her lie.

THE CULT OF BIRTHSTONES

THE FASHION for using 'birthstones' as personal amulets appears to have its origins in the twelve gemstones from the breastplate of the Jewish High-Priest and "the gems contributed for the tabernacle by the Israelists in the wilderness." There are two lists of twelve stones to be found in both the Old and New Testament but these do not correspond to the months of the year, or the Zodiac, but to the twelve tribes of Israel, or the twelve mighty angels who guard the gates of Paradise. The following extract is given in Exodus 28:15-30 and quoted in *The Curious Lore of Precious Stones*, written by that distinguished mineralogist George Frederick Kunz (1856-1932), who for more than 50 years was the gem expert for Tiffany's in New York:

... And thou shalt set in its [the breastplate] settings of stones, even four rows of stones: the first row shall be sardius [carnelian], a topaz, and a carbuncle; this shall be the first row.

And the second row shall be an emerald, a sapphire [lapis lazuli?] and a diamond [rock crystal or corundum?]

And the third row a ligure [amber or jacinth], an agate, and an amethyst.

And the fourth row a beryl, and an onyx, and a jasper; they shall be set in gold in their enclosings.

Islamic legend also represents the various heavens as composed of different precious stones, and in the Middle Ages these ideas became interwoven with a host of astrological, alchemical, magical and medical superstitions. There is, however, a much earlier Egyptian representation of the breast-ornament worn by a High-Priest of Memphis (14th Dynasty), consisting of twelve small balls or crosses. "As it cannot be determined that these figures were cut from precious stones, the only definite connection with the Hebrew ornament is the number of the figures; this suggests but fails to prove, a common origin," concluded Kunz.

Many of the 'classical' lists cited as antecedents for natal or zodiacal stones will include diamonds—but this gem could *not* have been one of the original stones simply because astrology dates back thousands of years and the ancient lapidaries did not know how to cut a diamond. It is possible that what was later mistaken for a diamond was more likely to have been rock crystal, but this 'humble' stone would not have been considered valuable enough in later times. The ancient priesthood, however, would have known about the magical powers contained within the rock crystal, even if latter day magicians did not.

Or as Kunz observed, "A mysterious stone mentioned three times in the Old Testament, each signifies a material noted for its hardness and translated 'diamond,' however, as it is almost certain that the Hebrews were not familiar with the 'diamond' it was most probably a variety of corundum..." Similarly, lapis lazuli was referred to as the 'sapphire of the ancients' and it may have been lapis rather than the rarer blue corundum that was in use at this time.

Birthstones are still used today as amulets to attract health, wealth and happiness, and most people know their own birthstone, but from the dozens of different compilations, which is the correct attribution for each month?

The cult of the birthstone and belief that each stone was endowed with its own peculiar virtue for those born in that month can be traced back to the writings of Josephus (1st century CE) and St Jerome (5th century). Despite these early references, the common usage of giving and wearing a birthstone seems to have originated much later in Poland sometime during the 18th century. The belief in the special virtues of the stones was paramount, and it was long before the mystic bond between the stone of the month, and the person born in that month was realized.

Nevertheless, nearly every book on gemstones will assign different stones for each month, and Kunz himself gives eight different listings from ancient Hebrew to the present day as examples. The following are taken from two contemporary publications on the subject—and even here there are contradictions for the given stones against each month.

Gemstones of the Month (*Spells, Charms, Talismans & Amulets*, Pamela A. Ball)

>January—Garnet, Onyx, Jet, Chrysoprase
>February—Amethyst, Jasper, Rock crystal
>March—Aquamarine, Bloodstone
>April—Ruby, Garnet, Sard
>May—Emerald, Malachite, Amber, Carnelian
>June—Topaz, Agate, Alexandrite, Fluorite

July—Moonstone, White agate

August—Cat's eye, Carnelian, Jasper, Fire agate

September—Peridot, Olivine, Chrysolite, Citrine

October—Opal, Tourmaline, Beryl, Turquoise

November—Topaz, Lapis lazuli

December—Serpentine, Jacinth, Peridot

Gemstones of the Zodiac (*Talismans, Charms & Amulets,* Robert W. Wood)

Aries—Red Jasper

Taurus—Rose Quartz

Gemini—Black Onyx

Cancer—Mother of Pearl

Leo—Tiger Eye

Virgo—Carnelian

Libra—Green Aventurine

Scorpio—Rhodonite

Sagittarius—Sodalite

Capricorn—Snowflake Obsidian

Aquarius—Blue Agate

Pisces—Amethyst

When looking for authenticity in terms of magical workings there is an additional complication caused by historical calendar re-alignments and what is known as precession. Because of the tidal effects of the Sun and Moon, the Earth 'wobbles' like a spinning top, causing the direction of the Vernal Equinox to shift in the sky. The early calendar makers were unaware of this phenomenon and believed that in making the beginning of the year dependent on the Sun's entry into the constellation of Aries, they were fixing it forever to the time of the Winter Solstice. At that ancient point in time, **theoretically the gemstone representing Aries would have been that of the *Winter Solstice,* i.e. December**.

As the centuries rolled by, the stars of Aries receded from the Winter Solstice, moving steadily through almost a quarter of the great ecliptic. By the 2nd century BCE, the Spring (or Vernal) Equinox was not far from the same point where the Winter Solstice had been when the first calendar-makers had fixed the constellation in the heavens. The Vernal Equinox is now on the cusp of Pisces and Aries but over the full 'wobble' it will move through all the signs in the Zodiac—**at the moment the gemstone for Aries is represented by that of the *Vernal Equinox*, i.e. March**.

There is also some evidence in favour of the theory that at the outset all twelve stones were acquired by the same person and worn in turn, each one during the respective month to which it was assigned, or during the ascendancy of its zodiacal sign. According to the German writer Bruckmann (1773, *Abhandlung von Edelsteinen*), "The stone of the month was believed to exercise its therapeutic (or

magical) virtue to the fullest extent during that period. Perhaps the fact that this entailed a monthly change of ornaments may rather have been a recommendation of the usage than the reverse."

When utilising gemstones as *magical* correspondences, however, it is vital we use the ancient propensities for each stone, because it is what the ancients believed and locks us into the universal subconsciousness so quintessential for successful magic. We are talking here of esoteric archetypes, not the fake-lore and fantasy of modern crystal working.

The twelve stones of the High-Priest's breastplate were sardius (carnelian), topaz, carbuncle, emerald, sapphire (lapis lazuli), diamond (corundum or rock crystal), ligure (amber or jacinth), agate, amethyst, beryl, onyx and jasper. Set in four rows of three to signify the seasons as suggested by Flavius Josephus and again by Clement of Alexandria in the 2nd century, they give us a starting point. Even then, things are not that simple. The 1539 CE edition of Marbodus' lapidary shows a figure of a High-Priest with the names and tribal attributions of the twelve stones, which differ slightly from the Greek Septuagint version from circa 250 BCE as follows—and shows where the confusion over the inclusion of the sapphire may have arisen.

1. Sardion (carnelian)—Odem
2. Topazion (topaz)—Pitdah
3. Smaragdus (carbuncle or emerald) —Bareketh
4. Anthrax (carbuncle or emerald)—Nophek
5. Sapphirus (lapis lazuli)— Sappir
6. Iaspis (corundum)—Yahalom
7. Ligurion (amber or jacinth)— Lesham
8. Achatâs (agate)—Shebo
9. Amethystos (amethyst)— Ahlamah
10. Chrysolithos (beryl or chalcedony)—Tarshish
11. Beryllion (beryl or onyx)— Shoham
12. Onychion (green jasper)— Yashpheh

The above does not claim to be the earliest, authentic list since there is still the suggestion that the Hebrew system may have been based on the earlier Egyptian version. Neither should we be dismissive of using an archaic Hebrew system as the foundation for our observances, for as any student of ritual magic will know, the Hebrew influence plays an important part in the development of the Western systems of practical Qabalah and ritual magic.

MELUSINE DRACO

MOON GARDENING

BY PHASE

Sow, transplant, bud and graft   *Plow, cultivate, weed and reap*

NEW	First Quarter	FULL	Last Quarter	NEW
Plant above-ground crops with outside seeds, flowering annuals.	Plant above-ground crops with inside seeds.	Plant root crops, bulbs, biennials, perennials.		Do not plant.

BY PLACE IN THE ZODIAC

In general—plant and transplant crops that bear above ground when the Moon is in a watery sign: Cancer, Scorpio or Pisces. Plant and transplant root crops when the Moon is in Taurus or Capricorn; the other earthy sign, Virgo, encourages rot. The airy signs, Gemini, Libra and Aquarius, are good for some crops and not for others. The fiery signs, Aries, Leo and Sagittarius, are barren signs for most crops and best used for weeding, pest control and cultivating the soil.

♈

Aries—*barren, hot and dry.* Favorable for planting and transplanting beets, onions and garlic, but unfavorable for all other crops. Good for weeding and pest control, for canning and preserving, and for all activities involving fire.

♉

Taurus—*fruitful, cold and dry.* Fertile, best for planting root crops and also very favorable for all transplanting as it encourages root growth. Good for planting crops that bear above ground and for canning and preserving. Prune in this sign to encourage root growth.

♊

Gemini—*barren, hot and moist.* The best sign for planting beans, which will bear more heavily. Unfavorable for other crops. Good for harvesting and for gathering herbs.

♋

Cancer—*fruitful, cold and moist.* Best for planting crops that bear above ground and very favorable for root crops. Dig garden beds when the Moon is in this sign, and everything planted in them will flourish. Prune in this sign to encourage growth.

♌

Leo—*barren, hot and dry.* Nothing should be planted or transplanted while the Moon is in the Lion. Favorable for weeding and pest control, for tilling and cultivating the soil, and for canning and preserving.

♍

Virgo—*barren, cold and dry.* Good for planting grasses and grains, but unfavorable for other crops. Unfavorable for canning and preserving, but favorable for weeding, pest control, tilling and cultivating. Make compost when the Moon is in the Virgin and it will ripen faster.

⚏

Libra—*fruitful, hot and moist*. The best sign to plant flowers and vines and somewhat favorable for crops that bear above the ground. Prune in this sign to encourage flowering.

♏

Scorpio—*fruitful, cold and moist*. Very favorable to plant and transplant crops that bear above ground, and favorable for planting and transplanting root crops. Set out fruit trees when the Moon is in this sign and prune to encourage growth.

♐

Sagittarius—*barren, hot and dry*. Favorable for planting onions, garlic and cucumbers, but unfavorable for all other crops, and especially unfavorable for transplanting. Favorable for canning and preserving, for tilling and cultivating the soil, and for pruning to discourage growth.

♑

Capricorn—*fruitful, cold and dry*. Very favorable for planting and transplanting root crops, favorable for flowers, vines, and all crops that bear above ground. Plant trees, bushes and vines in this sign. Prune trees and vines to strengthen the branches.

♒

Aquarius—*barren, hot and moist*. Favorable for weeding and pest control, tilling and cultivating the soil, harvesting crops, and gathering herbs. Somewhat favorable for planting crops that bear above ground, but only in dry weather or the seeds will tend to rot.

♓

Pisces—*fruitful, cold and moist*. Very favorable for planting and transplanting crops that bear above ground and favorable for flowers and all root crops except potatoes. Prune when the Moon is in the Fishes to encourage growth. Plant trees, bushes and vines in this sign.

Consult our Moon Calendar pages for phase and place in the zodiac circle. The Moon remains in a sign for about two and a half days. Match your gardening activity to the day that follows the Moon's entry into that zodiacal sign. For best results, choose days when the phase and sign are both favorable. For example, plant seeds when the Moon is waxing in a suitable fruitful sign, and uproot stubborn weeds when the Moon is in the fourth quarter in a barren sign.

The MOON Calendar

is divided into zodiac signs rather than the more familiar Gregorian calendar.

♈ 2020

♓ 2021

 Bear in mind that new projects should be initiated when the Moon is waxing (from dark to full). When the Moon is on the wane (from full to dark), it is a time for storing energy and the wise person waits.

Please note that Moons are listed by day of entry into each sign. Quarters are marked, but as rising and setting times vary from one region to another, it is advisable to check your local newspaper, library or planetarium.
The Moon's Place is computed for Eastern Time.

capricorn

December 21, 2019 – January 19, 2020
Cardinal Sign of Earth ▽ Ruled by Saturn ♄

S	M	T	W	T	F	S

						Dec. **21**
THE RAT: is a hardworking, intelligent type. They are absolutely independent and resolute in the process. They are not satisfied simply to accept anything at a face value; rather their inquisitiveness drives them to have a thorough knowledge of any situation. **CONTINUED**						Winter Solstice ❄ Scorpio

22	**23**	**24**	**25**	**26**	**27**	**28**
	Create a charm		Partial Solar Eclipse ⇨	●	WAXING	*Avoid nightmares*
	Sagittarius			Capricorn		Aquarius

29	**30**	**31**	Jan. **1**	**2**	**3**	**4**
Snap fingers three times			*Look both ways*	◗	*Eat an apple*	
	Pisces			Aries		Taurus

5	**6**	**7**	**8**	**9**	**10**	**11**
Test yourself			*Talk to the fey*	Feast of Janus	Storm Moon	WANING Partial Lunar Eclipse ⇦
		Gemini		Cancer		

12	**13**	**14**	**15**	**16**	**17**	**18**
	Engage a spirit		*Enjoy music*		◖	*Sleep*
Leo ⇦	Virgo		Libra			Scorpio

19	The Rat will watch for situations where they can take advantage. They usually act with speed and are flexible. While the Rat's curiosity can lead it into unsavory circumstance, they are escape artists. The downfall of Rats is they can over examine a situation. Their thrifty ways often devolve into miserly penny pinching. While easily driven to chattiness, the Rat in fact does not trust readily and is in a constant need of assurances that he is liked.

JANUS

January was named for Janus, the porter or janitor of heaven. He was the guardian deity of gateways, depicted as having two opposite faces, because every door looks two ways. Janus was a concept unknown to the Greeks, but from earliest times one held in high esteem by the Romans, who placed him on almost equal footing with Jupiter. The aid of both Gods was invoked prior to every understating. To Janus the Romans ascribed the origin of all things: the change of seasons, the ups and downs of fortune, and the civilization of the human race by means of agriculture, arts and religion. The heads of Janus are crowned with crescent Moon. He holds a key in his left hand to show it is within his power to unlock the future as well as lock away the past. The scepter in his right hand symbolizes his control of the progress of all undertakings. The public worship of Janus was introduced into Rome during the time of Numa Pompilius (715-672 BCE), but it seems likely that his conception as a deity is as old as the Rome of Romulus.

aquarius

January 20 – February 18, 2020
Fixed Sign of Air ♎ Ruled by Uranus ♅

S	M	T	W	T	F	S
牛 Sagittarius	Jan. **20**	**21**	**22** *Dance wildly* Capricorn	**23**	**24** Aquarius	Jan. **25** Chinese New Year Metal Rat
26 WAXING ⇦	**27** *Your beloved needs you* Pisces	**28**	**29** Aries	**30** *Call a friend*	**31** Oimelc Eve ⇨	Feb. **1** Taurus
2 Candlemas	**3** *Read the Tarot* Gemini	**4**	**5** *Temperance* Cancer	**6**	**7** Leo	**8** *Read an old almanac*
9 Chaste Moon	**10** WANING Virgo	**11**	**12** *Gather snow* Libra	**13**	**14** Lupercalia ⇨ Scorpio	**15**
16 *Wolves howl* Sagittarius	**17**	**18** Capricorn	**THE OX:** They are hardworking, diligent and can stick to an arduous task longer than most. They often put their heart into the job at hand and will dive into a project with vigor that outstrips their colleagues. In the Ox you will find a fiercely loyal partner and friend. In fact, in their			

book the breaching of loyalty is the most egregious offense. The Ox puts family and friends above all. While they take their time in committing to a situation, they will be unwavering in dedication once the decision has been made. The Ox can indeed be a bit on the stubborn side and fixated on a single issue, sticking to rules even if they become an impediment to progress. They also have a temper that is quick to flare, always needing space and time to calm down.

High Magic's Aid is one of the early classic books written by Gerald Gardner, the father of Modern Wicca. He would often give prospective students a copy, gaging the fitness for his teaching by their reaction to the content.

pisces

February 19 – March 19, 2020

Mutable Sign of Water ▽ *Ruled by Neptune* ♆

S	M	T	W	T	F	S
THE TIGER: They are born leaders, always exhibiting an air of authority, acting courageously and proudly. They are among the most irresistible, with many being attracted to **CONTINUED**			Feb. **19**	**20** Aquarius	**21**	**22** *Question the dead*
23 ● Pisces	**24** WAXING Aries	**25**	**26** . *Rest the mind*	**27**	**28** *Find what you lost* Taurus	**29** Leap Day
Mar. **1** Matronalia Gemini	**2** ◗	**3** *Relay a message*	**4** Cancer	**5**	**6** *Express passion* Leo	**7**
8 *Drink water* Virgo	**9** ○	**10** WANING Libra	**11**	**12** *Bury a curse* Scorpio	**13**	**14** *Draw with color* Sagittarius
15 *Trust the garden*	**16** ◖	**17** Capricorn	**18** *Don't tempt fate*	**19** *Minerva's Day* Aquarius		

their magnetic personality. The Tiger is calm and warmhearted, but can be tempestuous and terrifying if necessary. The Tiger has an essential need to be dominant in their group. If this need is not met, they can easily become depressed. The Tiger often will act quickly when presented with a task; they will plunge headlong into action without thought. They are often more abrupt and hasty than their peers. Tigers will rebel against authority just to make their point known.

"WE HAVE CEASED to believe in a mystical soul-substance which was formerly supposed to inhabit the body as a stranger, and which after death will hover about somewhere as a spectre. We have ceased to believe in ghosts; science has banished the phantoms of disembodied spirits out of the provinces of psychology and philosophy. But must we for that reason cease to believe in life and in spiritual life? Must we therefore consider death as a finality? Does not science teach the persistence of life and of spiritual life; and is there the slightest reason that we should cease to believe in the immortality of our ideals? Is it not a fact, scientifically indubitable, that every work done, be it good or evil, continues in its effects upon future events? Is it not a fact established upon reliable observations that the evolution of mankind, and of all life generally upon earth, is one great and continuous whole; that even to-day the efforts of our ancestors are preserved in the present generation; their features, their characters, their souls now live in us. Certainly not all features are preserved, but those only which nature considered worth preserving. So our characters, our thoughts, our aspirations, our souls will live in future generations, if they are strong enough, if they are noble and elevating. In order to be strong, they must be in accord with nature, they must be true. In order to live, they must be engendered by the evolutionary tendency in nature, which constantly endeavors to lift life to higher planes. It must be, as the Christian expresses it, in harmony with God, if God is meant to be that power in nature and in our hearts that ever again and again prompts us to struggle and to strive for something higher."

—*Homilies of Science* BY DR. PAUL CARUS, CHICAGO, 1892

aries

March 20 – April 19, 2020
Cardinal Sign of Fire △ Ruled by Mars ♂

S	M	T	W	T	F	S
DIAMOND the stone of eternity has an unconquerable hardness. The diamond takes its name from *adamas* meaning invincible. It is no wonder that those who bear a diamond will have the benefit of heightened strength, invincibility and courage. This rare stone known for its beauty, has been ⬇				Mar **19** Vernal Equinox Aquarius	**20** *Power in* *passion*	**21** Pisces
22 *Wear gold*	**23**	**24** ⚫ Aries	**25** WAXING	**26** *Extra effort* Taurus	**27**	**28** *Talk to a* *mirror* Gemini
29	**30** *Meet* *friends*	**31** April Fools Day ⇨ Cancer	April **1** ◑	**2** Leo	**3** *Start a* *project*	**4** Virgo
5 *Add honey*	**6** Libra	**7** Seed Moon	**8** WANING Scorpio	**9** *Meditate*	**10** Sagittarius	**11** *Play hard*
12 Capricorn	**13** *Ask for* *opinions*	**14** ◑	**15** *Do the* *possible* Aquarius	**16**	**17** *Help some-* *one finish* Pisces	**18**
19	a symbol of innocence and love. Diamond's high frequency results from the synthesis of all. The diamond activates the crown chakra connecting flesh with spirit. It is the stone of perfection achieved when there is a synthesis of the higher self with the lower self. Diamonds can be imbibed by drinking water in which a diamond has steeped.					

The Geomantic Figures: Amissio

GEOMANCY IS AN ANCIENT SYSTEM of divination that uses sixteen symbols, the geomantic figures. Easy to learn and use, it was one of the most popular divination methods in the Middle Ages and Renaissance. It remained in use among rural cunning folk for many centuries thereafter, and is now undergoing a renaissance of its own as diviners discover its possibilities.

The geomantic figures are made up of single and double dots. Each figure has a name and a divinatory meaning, and the figures are also assigned to the four elements, the twelve signs of the Zodiac, the seven planets and the nodes of the Moon. The dots that make up the figures signify their inner meanings: the four lines of dots represent Fire, Air, Water and Earth and show that the elements are present in either active (one dot) or latent (two dots) form.

The second of the geomantic figures is Amissio (pronounced ah-MISH-ee-oh), which means Loss. It belongs to the element of Earth, the Zodiacal sign Taurus, and the planet Venus. The arrangement of dots in Amissio symbolize a bag or jug turned upside down so that the contents fall out.

Read as symbols of the elements, the dots that form Amissio reveal much about the nature of this figure. The uppermost line, with one dot, shows that Fire is present in active form; the single dot in the third line shows that Water is in the same active state. The second and fourth lines, which stand for Air and Earth, show that these elements are inactive or latent. Without Air to link them together or

Earth to give them a stable basis, Fire and Water can't remain in contact for long—either the Water puts out the Fire or the Fire boils off the water.

In divination Amissio is an unfavorable omen in any reading having to do with money or property. In readings about love or health, however, it is an excellent sign. Does that seem counterintuitive? Love affairs go better when you let go of your ego and lose your heart, and healing is very often a matter of letting go of harmful behavior patterns or toxins trapped in the body. More generally, whenever you need to lose something, to let something go, or to let things happen in their own way, Amissio is a favorable sign.

—JOHN MICHAEL GREER

taurus

April 20 – May 20, 2020

Fixed Sign of Earth ☿ Ruled by Venus ♀

S	M	T	W	T	F	S
	April **20** Yield to the point Aries	**21**	**22** Taurus	**23** WAXING	**24** Remember when	**25** Gemini
26 Be reliable	**27** Cancer	**28** Tackle a family issue	**29** Walpurgis Night ⇨	**30** Leo	May **1** Beltane	**2** Give something special Virgo
3 Plan some fun	**4** Libra	**5** Break the mold	**6** Vesak Day ⇨ Scorpio	**7** Hare Moon	**8** White Lotus Day WANING Sagittarius	**9** Skip a meal
10 Capricorn	**11** Write it out	**12** Aquarius	**13** Check your horoscope	**14**	**15** Hold hands Pisces	**16**
17 Aries	**18** Apologize	**19**	**20** Puzzles Taurus			

EMERALD is known as the stone of success. Its name has its origin in the Sanskrit word *merkata* meaning the green of plant growth. The varieties of green that emeralds manifest point to the many possibilities of renewal that are always present. Emerald is a stone said to promote good business by imbuing the bearer with a statured presence and eloquent communication. It has a long association with Hermes/Mercury and the inner mysteries. It is said that Hermes Trismegistus set down his principles on emerald tablets. Those who carry emerald may find they have enhanced revelations of truth. Emerald also has a long association with Venus, imparting security through love. It is associated with the heart chakra. Emerald is one of the four precious stones.

Notable Quotations

STONES

There is amongst them the gentler fire of the ruby, there is the rich purple of the amethyst, there is the sea-green of the emerald, and all shining together in an indescribable union. Others, by an excessive heightening of their hues equal all the colors of the painter, others the flame of burning brimstone, or of a fire quickened by oil.

−Pliny the Elder

River stones remain, while water flows away.

−Romanian

You have to have the right sort of stone. Peridot for mothers, girasol for lovers, sapphire for sadness, and garnet for joy."

−Catherynne M. Valente
The Girl Who Soared Over Fairyland and Cut the Moon in Two

I adore wearing gems, but not because they are mine. You can't possess radiance, you can only admire it.

−Elizabeth Taylor

We should build with the stones we have.

−Swedish

Everything dreams. The play of form, of being, is the dreaming of substance. Rocks have their dreams, and the earth changes…

−Ursula K. Le Guin
The Lathe of Heaven

The cutting of the gem has to be finished before you can see whether it shines.

−Leonard Cohen

If it weren't for the rocks in its bed, the stream would have no song.

−Carl Perkins

Crystals grew inside rock like arithmetical flowers. They lengthened and spread, adding plane to plane in awed and perfect obedience to an absolute geometry that even the stones—maybe only the stones—understood.

−Annie Dillard
An American Childhood

Quotes compiled by Isabel Kunkle

gemini

May 21 – June 20, 2020

Mutable Sign of Air △ Ruled by Mercury ☿

S	M	T	W	T	F	S
MOONSTONE is the stone of meditation. The shimmering colors of moonstone are a result of the combination of light and mineral. This quality imbues it with an ability to reflect and synchronize with inner energies and rhythms, providing a soothing effect. Moonstones act as creativity. ⬇				May **21** *Take charge*	**22** ● Gemini	**23** WAXING
24 Cancer	**25** *Trust your feelings*	**26**	**27** Leo	**28** *Say it differently*	**29** ◑ Virgo	**30** Oak Apple Day ⇐
31 *Ask why* Libra	June **1**	**2** *Let it out* Scorpio	**3** *Learn a trick*	**4** Partial Lunar Eclipse ⇒ Sagittarius	**5** ◯ Dyad Moon	**6** Watchers ⇐ WANING Capricorn
7 *Appreciate good work*	**8** Aquarius	**9**	**10** Look *it up*	**11** Pisces	**12** *Connect with children*	**13** ◑ Aries
14 *Dress loud*	**15**	**16** *Wrap it up* Taurus	**17**	**18** *Think about feelings* Gemini	**19**	**20** Summer Solstice

Its association with the Moon and natural rhythms make this a good stone to mitigate hormonal and psychological discord. Moonstones are also known as the traveler's stone. It can have a soothing effect on those who have a propensity toward road rage. Moonstone is a good amulet to keep in the car, as well as to carry on your person when traveling.

TAROT'S THE MOON

THE SECOND CELESTIAL TRUMP in our deck follows the Conver design. The Moon is depicted here alone in the sky, letting what appear to be drops of dew fall into a dew pond. Out of this arises a crayfish or crab, the astrological symbol for Cancer and zodiacal house by which the Moon is ruled. Flanked by two towers and baying dogs that seem to represent the binary powers of light and darkness, the Moon's positioning here in the trump sequence precedes the Sun and indicates the imminent arrival of the penultimate card, the Last Judgment—the final drama in the liturgical cycle. Isaiah 30:26 alludes to this moment: "The moon shall shine with a brightness like the sun's... on the day when the Lord binds up the broken limbs of his people and heals their wounds." Aside from being a source of moisture, lunacy and plant growth, the Moon was also considered by Renaissance philosophers to be the force behind dreams and sleep, as well as the phenomenon of flux and reflux: the ocean's tides, the red tide of the human bloodstream, a woman's menstrual cycle, and ultimately anything like the Moon that waxes and wanes and is periodically cyclic. Cartomancers bear all these considerations in mind when interpreting this card.

Excerpted from Dame Fortune's Wheel Tarot—A Pictorial Key *by Paul Huson, published by The Witches' Almanac.*

cancer
June 21 – July 22, 2020
Cardinal Sign of Water ▽ Ruled by Moon ☽

CANCER

S	M	T	W	T	F	S
June **21** ● Cancer	**22** WAXING Partial Solar Eclipse ⇦	**23** *Commit* Leo	**24** Midsummer	**25** Virgo	**26** *Share*	**27** Libra
28 ◑	**29** *Look up* Scorpio	**30**	July **1** *Plan big* Sagittarius	**2**	**3** Capricorn	**4** *See the water* Partial Lunar Eclipse ⇨
5 (Mead Moon)	**6** WANING Aquarius	**7** *Challenge authority*	**8** Pisces	**9** *Reorganize*	**10**	**11** *Reconsider* Aries
12 ◐	**13** *Slow down* Taurus	**14**	**15** *Get a book*	**16** Gemini	**17**	**18** *Go out* Cancer
19	**20** ● Leo	**21** *Research a dream*	**22** WAXING Virgo			

RUBY was described as a drop of the Mother Earth's blood in the ancient far east. Associated with royalty, to gift Krishna one of these precious stones was an assurance of being born royal in the next life.

Ruby's name comes to us from the Latin *ruber* meaning red. The redness of the ruby imparts strength. Associated with the Sun, the ruby is a symbol of passion and potency. The wearer has been advised in the past to pay attention as darkening of the stone is a warning of danger. Many have used it to awaken the kundalini and connect to their heart chakra, opening it for new experiences of love: spiritual, corporal and self.

The *Queen of the Night* Relief
Identified by some as Lilith

leo

July 23 – August 22, 2020

Fixed Sign of Fire △ Ruled by Sun ☉

LEO

S	M	T	W	T	F	S
PERIDOT baptized in the fires of volcanoes; this stone radiates pure energy when held. The Romans called this stone Evening Emerald, its history running deep in ancient Mediterranean culture. Peridot was thought as a revitalizing stone, dispelling darker emotions, easing the bearer into calmer states. ↓				July **23** Ancient Egyptian New Year	**24** *Acknowledge support* Libra	**25**
26 *Yes*	**27** Scorpio	**28**	**29** *Consider a tree* Sagittarius	**30**	**31** Lughnassad Eve Capricorn	Aug **1** Lammas
2 *Give a gift* Aquarius	**3** Wort Moon	**4** WANING	**5** Pisces	**6** *Make peace*	**7** Aries	**8**
9 *Toss a penny* Taurus	**10**	**11**	**12** *Tie a knot* Gemini	**13** Diana's Day	**14** Cancer	**15** *Treat yourself*
16	**17** Black Cat Appreciation Day Leo	**18**	**19** WAXING Virgo	**20**	**21** *Light a pink candle* Libra	**22** Ganesha Chaturthi

Its bright green inspires an optimism and overall wellbeing. Peridot is said to be a stone that connects the Earth and the Sun and is well used to tread the astral path between the two. To the pharaonic Egyptians, it was a solar stone to be worn by the pharaoh during ritual occasions. Its strong vibration protects the bearer during the day and more importantly protects against the terrors of the night.

⋛ Elder ⋜

RUIS

THE ELDER TREE of northern Europe once had a resident deity of magical significance that has lasted through the centuries. Scandinavian legends tell of the Elder Mother watching for any injury to the tree. If even a sprig is cut without first asking permission of the Elder Mother, whatever purpose the sprig is cut for will end in misfortune.

Once permission has been asked and a twig of the elder tree secured, it will banish evil spirits and may be hung or worn as an amulet. Elder flowers, dried while the Moon waxes from dark to full, are a potent love charm. The berries gathered at Summer Solstice afford protection from all unexpected dangers, including accidents and lightning strikes.

Beyond its subtle gifts, the elder offers healing for a variety of ailments. Its leaves are an effective insect repellent; its close-grained wood finds favor with carpenters; its berries provide a deep purple dye as well as culinary treats and the renowned elderberry wine.

Reverence for the Elder Mother challenged the early Christian church who redefined the tree Goddess as a wicked Witch more to be feared then adored, believing the Elder to be the tree of Christ's crucifiction. To place a baby in an elder cradle invited an evil spirit to come and snuff out its life. The tree constituted so serious a threat that England's King Edgar in the tenth century issued a warning against "those vein practices which are carried on with elders."

Folklore passed down to us today reflects these ambivalent attitudes, for elders are more often considered evil than good. Only in Denmark has the Elder Mother, Hylde-Moer, retained her sacred nature. Hans Christian Andersen's tale of the Elder Mother who becomes a beautiful maiden named Memory captures the spirit of the most ancient lore.

virgo
August 23 – September 22, 2020
Mutable Sign of Earth ⊽ Ruled by Mercury ☿

S	M	T	W	T	F	S
Aug. **23** Scorpio	**24** *Give it back*	**25** Sagittarius	**26** *Call it done*	**27** Capricorn	**28**	**29** *New plan* Aquarius
30	**31**	Sept. **1** *Make some-thing* Pisces	**2** Barley Moon	**3** WANING Aries	**4** *Read to someone*	**5**
6 *Stay on track* Taurus	**7**	**8** *Do it different* Gemini	**9**	**10**	**11** Cancer	**12** *Stack rocks*
13 Ganesh Festival Leo	**14** *Find a leaf*	**15** Virgo	**16** *Be wary*	**17** Libra	**18** WAXING	**19** Scorpio
20 *Share a poem*	**21** Sagittarius					

SAPPHIRE is the gem of wisdom and magnificence. This stone has been used since time immemorial to enhance knowledge and to give its bearer clear sight. Sapphire is said to promote learning, as well as perception and understanding. It is said to wear a sapphire is to attract divine blessing. Sapphires stimulate the throat chakra and the third eye, allowing the bearer to contact with levels of consciousness expressed in dream and symbol. A person in a leadership position can benefit from the fair administration of pressure and ability to focus a group that Sapphires may impart. Protection from sorcery and maleficent thoughts is a well sought-after virtue of this bluest of stones.

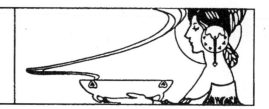

Bean Fritters

COOKING FOR THE ORIṢÁ. Food is a integral component of the ritual and offerings for the deities of the Yorùbá both in Yorùbáland and the diaspora. The initiations of a new priest of any given Oriṣá is usually attended by many priests, diviners, family members and drummers. The celebrations that ensue on the subsequent evenings are joyous and typically last into the wee hours of the morning.

A common food that is enjoyed by man and deity alike is the black eyed bean fritter known as *akara*. Traditionally it is a food that is served for breakfast. It can be found where ever the Yorùbá have come to live and is often an afternoon snack item. For example, you would be hard pressed to walk the streets of Rio de Janeiro, Brazil without coming across a street vendor selling these delicious morsels.

For these tasty, deep-fried cakes, you need only five items:

1 cup of beans (black-eyed beans)
2 habanero peppers (also chilli peppers)
1 medium onion
Salt to taste
Vegetable oil for frying (palm oil is traditional)

The preparation for akara begins with the soaking of the beans and removing the bean coat. The beans should be soaked for approximately two hours. You can test if they have been soaked long enough by rubbing two beans together, if the coat comes of with ease, they are all ready to be shucked.

The beans should be placed in the blender only adding water to keep the blades going. Once the beans have been puréed, they will need to be whipped by hand. The whipping is to get air bubbles into the batter. The batter will turn white when air is infused throughout.

The oil should be heated at this point. There should be enough oil to cover your fritter (approximately 3").

When the oil has reached the point of boiling, add the finely chopped onion and peppers. The salt should only be added a moment before you begin to drop the fritters into the oil. The fritters should be fried until they are golden brown. They should be placed either in a sieve or on paper towel to remove the excess oil. They can be lightly salted to taste before eating. Enjoy, and be sure to share with the Oriṣá!

—IFADOYIN SANGOMUYIWA

libra

September 23 – October 22, 2020

Cardinal Sign of Air ♎ Ruled by Venus ♀

LIBRA

S	M	T	W	T	F	S
OPAL is a stone that is said to bring the aura in to attunement. Opal coming from the Sanskrit word *upala* meaning "precious ↓	Sept. **22** Autumnal Equinox ♑ Capricorn	**23** Capricorn	**24**	**25** *Share a secret*	**26** Aquarius	
27	**28** *Stop gossip* Pisces	**29**	**30** *Use your strength* Aries	Oct. **1** Blood Moon	**2** WANING	**3** Taurus
4 *Gratitude*	**5**	**6** *Forgive yourself* Gemini	**7**	**8** *Use a process* Cancer	**9**	**10** Leo
11	**12** *Details matter* Virgo	**13**	**14**	**15** *Share your peace* Libra	**16**	**17** WAXING Scorpio
18 *Make it work*	**19** Sagittarius	**20**	**21** *Add on* Capricorn	**22**		

stone," its flashing colors clear the aura allowing the bearer to work on deep levels of being and cosmic consciousness. A prophecy enhancer, its genesis is in Greek myth. It is said that Zeus cried tears of opal after he defeated the Titans. The quality of the opal boosts psychic centers. Opal amplifies traits, extending to both light and dark. Before working the opal, grounding is always recommended. The colors of opal connect it to the seven rays of the chakras. It has been said that opal can make the bearer invisible;

Saul consulting the spirit of Samuel after the witch of Endor has conjured him from the dead

scorpio

October 23 – November 21, 2020
Fixed Sign of Water ▽ Ruled by Pluto♀

SCORPIVS

S	M	T	W	T	F	S
CITRINE is a very solar stone, having many uses throughout ancient Aegean culture. The pharaohs were buried with citrine jewellery understanding that this beautiful gem would help the pharaoh in the afterlife. Like sunlight piercing the spring sky, ↓					Oct **23** Aquarius	**24** *Celebrate*
25 Pisces	**26**	**27**. *Almost is enough*	**28** Aries	**29** *Know your part*	**30** Samhain Eve ⇨ Taurus	**31** Snow Moon
Nov. **1** Hallowmas WANING	**2** *Consider the other side* Gemini	**3**	**4** *Tarot* Cancer	**5**	**6**	**7** *Be firm* Leo
8	**9** *Accept change* Virgo	**10**	**11** *Bring them together* Libra	**12**	**13** Scorpio	**14** *Manifest*
15 Sagittarius	**16** Hecate Night WAXING	**17** *Midnight Oil* Capricorn	**18**	**19** *Ritual for change* Aquarius	**20**	**21**

citrine has an ability to clear the mind and incite the bearer to move into action. Artists benefit from citrine's ability to awaken the creative process, helping to transform dreams and visions into reality. Rather than generating energy, citrine acts as transformer. During times of stress, citrine can be used to transform negative energies into positive. A bit of citrine in the cash register just may see an increase of income or sales. It is also a good stone to work with before making investments. Citrine's golden color makes it a stone of commerce.

Victorian Slang

Gas-Pipes—really tight pants

Bricky—brave or fearless

Mafficking—getting rowdy in the streets

Butter upon bacon—extravagance

Half-rats—partially drunk

Gal-sneaker—a seduction of women

Church-bell—a talkative woman

Chuckaboo—what you call a close friend

Gigglemug—habitual smiling face

Got the morbs—mildly depressed

Mad as hops—excitable

Not up to dick—feeling unwell

Podsnappery—a refusal to recognize unpleasant facts

Daddles—hands

Damfino—damned if I know

Don't sell me a dog—don't lie to me

Fly rink—a polished bald head

Poked up—embarrassed

Sauce-box—a mouth

Bitch the pot—pour the tea

Tight as a boiled owl—drunk

Tallywags—testicles

Cupids kettle drums—boobs

Bubbies—boobs

Beer and skittles—good times

Made that—hold your tongue

Nice thin job—evasion of a promise

Git-a-bit—obtaining money

sagittarius

November 22 – December 21, 2020

Mutable Sign of Fire △ Ruled by Jupiter ♃

S	M	T	W	T	F	S
Nov. **22** Pisces	**23** *Make a sigil*	**24** Aries	**25** *Push your luck*	**26**	**27** *Lessons learned* Taurus	**28**
29 Partial Lunar Eclipse ⇨ Gemini	**30** Oak Moon	Dec. **1** WANING	**2** *Reconnect* Cancer	**3**	**4** Leo	**5** *Big changes*
Dec. **6** Virgo	**7**	**8** *Share success* Libra	**9**	**10** *Wield charity* Scorpio	**11**	**12** *Make a wish* Sagittarius
13 Total Solar Eclipse ⇨	**14**	**15** WAXING Capricorn	**16** Fairy Queen Eve	**17** Saturnalia Aquarius	**18** *Soul food*	**19** Pisces

20 — **TANZANITE** the stone of the Third Eye Chakra, is the perfect stone for developing psychic abilities. Paired with the protective qualities that it has, tanzanite allows those wearing it to enter into altered states and assists the traveller in pathworking. It is believed that even the smallest stone will enhance the bearer's ability to communicate clearly. Tanzanite is said to dispel lethargy and is a good stone for escaping the grip of inertia, both physically and spiritually. Working with it, compassion and spiritual love deepen. Tanzanite's ability to help with the healing of somatised emotions makes it unique among the stones used for healing. Some have used tanzanite to help in dealing with headaches and migraines. For those looking to turn to their inner landscape, its use as an agent of wisdom and truth can have a profound affect on those using tanzanite as an aid to meditation.

YEAR OF THE METAL RAT
January 25, 2020–February 12, 2021

THE RAT IS REVERED throughout the Orient for his craftiness and charm. Buddha gifted the Rat with the first sign in this, the world's oldest zodiac, which follows a twelve-year cycle where each year is named for one of the twelve animals at Buddha's gathering. It also incorporates five elements: fire, water, wood, metal and earth. Each sixty years the element-animal pairs repeat. Chinese New Year begins in late January to mid-February, at the time of the New Moon in Aquarius.

An emotional and idealistic mood prevails during a Metal Rat year. This is a White Rat who will support liberal philosophies. Something of the pack rat prevails. Many will seek collectibles to purchase and stock up on bargain items.

Personality Profile
The Metal or White Rat succeeds through clever networking and making influential contacts. Charming, protective, compassionate, loving and talented, this Rat is a gifted troubleshooter who seeks acceptance and peace. Years of the Rat are considered very auspicious for a birthday. If you are a Rat, you are described as creative, gracious, a good advisor and classy. Loyalty and a strong sense of justice round out your exceptional character.

More information on the Metal Rat can be found on our website at
http://TheWitchesAlmanac.com/Almanac-Extras/

Years of the Rat
1936, 1948, 1960, 1972, 1984, 1996, 2008, 2020, 2032

Illustration by Ogmios MacMerlin

capricorn

December 21 2020 – January 19, 2021
Cardinal Sign of Earth ♀ Ruled by Saturn ♄

S	M	T	W	T	F	S
	Dec **21** Aries	**22** Winter Solstice ❄ ⇦	**23**	**24** *Be gracious* Taurus	**25**	Dec **26** *Be patient* Gemini
27	**28** *Guard what is yours*	**29** Wolf Moon Cancer	**30** WANING	**31** *Guard it more* Leo	Jan. **1**	**2** *Ask a favor* Virgo
3	**4**	**5** *Share the work* Libra	**6**	**7** Scorpio	**8** *Enjoy relatives*	**9** Feast of Janus Sagittarius
10	**11** *Organize finances* Capricorn	**12**	**13** Aquarius	**14** WAXING	**15** Pisces	**16** *Invest*
17	**18** *Reflect on success* Aries	**19**				

GARNET is one of the most ancient precious stones known to mankind. While most associate garnet with the commonly know red fiery stone, it can however form in a number of colors. Taking its name from the Latin *granatus* meaning seed-like, the common red is the color likened to pomegranate seeds. It is linked with the root chakra, as well as the heart chakra. Garnet is said to fend off melancholy and is a stimulant for the heart. The wearer should pay attention to the luster of the stone, as cloudiness can indicate coming problems. In carrying or wearing garnet, there is heightened ability to focus increasing determination and an impetus to attain goals. Garnet is a good stone for the business man providing clarity of thought and courage, as well as increasing attractiveness.

Senbazuru

One Thousand Origami Cranes

The origins of origami have been lost in the annals of time. It is likely that it followed shortly on the heels of paper arriving on the shores of Japan circa 105 CE. While present day origami is an arts and crafts recreation activity, initially it was a ceremonial act.

The iconic origami crane has a special place among the many items that can be fashioned by folding paper. The crane is a mystical creature in Japanese, Korean and Chinese cultures. It was believed that cranes lived for a thousand years and have been held in high esteem. They represent good fortune and longevity.

The folding of 1,000 origami cranes is called Senbazuru (*sen* meaning 1,000, *orizuru* meaning cranes.) Legend has it that any who would make one crane for each of its years of life will be blessed with one wish by the crane. There are also legends that folding 1,000 cranes can grant luck, long life or recovery from an injury or illness. Many of the legends advise that the cranes must be made and strung in a period no longer than a year.

The gifting of Senbazuru to the sick is a common practice. There is also a tradition of gifting them to newly married couples. In any case the cranes are usually made in a variety of colors. Instructions for construction of cranes can be found at TheWitchesAlmanac. com/almanac-extras/.

—DEVON STRONG

aquarius

January 20 – February 18, 2021
Fixed Sign of Air △ Ruled by Uranus ♅

S	M	T	W	T	F	S
AMETHYST's meaning is rooted in the Greek word *methysménos* meaning drunken. This points to the Greek myth of a young virgin named Amethyst. A very drunk Dionysus became enamoured with her. As a ↓			Jan. **20** ◑ Taurus	**21** *No status quo*	**22**	**23** *Spontaneity* Gemini
24 Chinese New Year Year of the Rat ⇨	**25** *Breathe* Cancer	**26**	**27** *Consider your image* Leo	**28** Storm Moon ○	**29** WANING	Feb. **30** Virgo
31 *Eat something new*	Feb. **1** Oimelc Eve Libra	**2** Candlemas	**3** *Go deeper* Scorpio	**4** ◑	**5** *Flirty fun* Sagittarius	**6**
7 *Turn it up*	**8** Carpricorn	**9** *Another way*	**10** Aquarius	**11** ●	**12** *Share tea* Pisces	**13** WAXING
14 *Break the chains* Aries	**15** Lupercalia	**16** *Burn incense*	**17** *Give advice* Taurus	**18**		

result of Amethyst's plea for help, Diana turned her into a brilliant white stone. Dionysus in his sorrow, spilled his goblet of wine on the stone, which from that day was purple. Carrying amethyst is said to encourage a sober mind. It has an effect on the pineal gland which is the root of altered states and psychic occurrences, allowing for an ability to prophesize and receive visions. Amethyst is connected with the crown chakra, the spot where divinity is essence touches the soul of mankind. Many also use it to guard against anger and overzealous passion.

Mount, water, to the skies!
Bid the sudden storm arise.
Bid the pitchy clouds advance,
Bid the forked lightnings glance,
Bid the angry thunder growl,
Bid the wild wind fiercely howl!
Bid the tempest come amain,
Thunder, lightning, wind, and rain!

As she concluded, clouds gathered thickly overhead, obscuring the stars that had hitherto shone down from the heavens. The wind suddenly arose, but in lieu of dispersing the vapours, it seemed only to condense them. A flash of forked lightning cut through the air, and a loud peal of thunder rolled overhead.

Then the whole troop sang together —

Beat the water, Demdike's daughter!
See the tempest gathers o'er us;
Lightning flashes — thunder crashes,
Wild winds sing in lusty chorus!

The Lancashire Witches,
by William Harrison Ainsworth (1848)

pisces

February 19 – March 20, 2021

Mutable Sign of Water ▽ Ruled by Neptune ♆

S	M	T	W	T	F	S
AQUAMARINE shimmers blue, green and white just like the sea water it is named for. Since ancient times, it has been the stone of sailors who carried it for safe passage and as a safeguard against drowning. It can imbue the bearer with a sense of calm, and its soothing quality can be directed at abating fear. Aquamarine is a stone that works with the ↓					Feb **19** ◐ Gemini	**20** *Collaborate*
21 *Journey through art*	**22** Cancer	**23**	**24** *Show how* Leo	Mar. **25**	**26** Virgo	**27** Chaste Moon
28 WANING Libra	Mar. **1** Matronalia	**2** *Be gentle* Scorpio	**3**	**4** *See what is* Sagittarius	**5** ◐	**6** *Do it* Capricorn
7	**8** *Watch the sky*	**9** Aquarius	**10**	**11** *Support charity* Pisces	**12**	**13** ● Aries
14 WAXING	**15** *Find the good*	**16** Taurus	**17**	**18** *Use words* Gemini	**19** Minerva's Day	**20** *Have faith*

throat chakra, being used for general health and wellness in the thyroid and larynx. Placing the stone in water for a time and then drinking the water is said to aid the body, mind and spirit. Aquamarine also has many spiritual qualities. In the past, it was believed shewstones of aquamarine made for easier communications with spirits. Its ability to calm the mind makes it a good tool for communication with the higher realms.

Legends of the Fairy Cross

FEW OF THE various legends told throughout the ages about stones and gems are so beautiful and poignant as that of the remarkable mineral known as staurolite, (from the Greek words *stauros* for cross and *lithos* for stone), commonly called the fairy cross. These singular stones of aluminum, iron and silica form either perfect cross-like structures or right angles. They can resemble the Celtic, Roman, Maltese, and St. Andrew's crosses. Perfect specimens are rare and highly prized by mystics and collectors. Often those sold have been filed from the matrix and then repaired with clay or even simulated. Usually fairy crosses are a dark opaque reddish brown or black in color, an inch or so in length. Sometimes artisans will polish especially nice specimens and mount them in gold to create talismans which become precious jewelry.

For hundreds of years fairy crosses have been carried as lucky charms to ward off bad luck in the form of evil doers, ill health, accidents and natural disasters. It is even rumored that at least three United States Presidents, including Theodore Roosevelt and Woodrow Wilson, as well as other historic figures, have carried these powerful talismans.

A traditional Native American ancestor story relates fairy crosses to teardrops shed by the Yunwi Tsunsdi. These tiny fairy spirits are sensitive, elusive and timid. They are helpful, though, especially when called upon to locate lost people. As is usual with the Little People they were at a celebration one evening which included songs and dances. Suddenly a foreign messenger arrived, bringing the sorrowful account of the Crucifixion. This horrible story caused the Wee Folk to weep and weep. Their falling tears became small stone crosses which covered the ground. Since cross talismans as sacred symbols predate the introduction of Christianity to the

indigenous people by at least 12,000 years, perhaps this particular legend of Christ and the Crucifixion veils a deeper sorrow, acknowledging their lost way of life.

By some accounts the fairy spirits were never seen again following the sad interruption of their party. Others say their whispers can be heard still in the sighs of gentle breezes along the riverfront and in the tree tops.

Cherokee elders sometimes tell of how the fairy cross will give the bearer the gift of invisibility at will. Others say the talismans will reward good and kind actions. A more sinister power associated with these intriguing stones is that they give the bearer an ability to travel underground and surface amid the enemy. This brings an advantage in battle, allowing them to surprise, frighten and overcome adversaries.

In contemporary metaphysical teachings the fairy cross has been linked to the root and crown chakras. Their attributes include recovery, healing and practicality. Fairy crosses are thought to carry Earth's nurturing forces and bring a reminder to honor the planet. They enhance meditation and will attract practical solutions to everyday problems, thus becoming a prosperity stone. Fairy crosses are also credited with highlighting psychic insights, especially in regard to grounding and clarity. Some say that fairy crosses will adopt the owner instead of the other way around and that they forge a connection with the Little People.

Overall fairy crosses are used in modern witchery to promote a positive mindset and upbeat emotional state. They are credited with helping trauma victims. The fairy cross is thought to bring a positive spin on undesirable situations. Their energy is calming and seems to quell angry, negative feelings.

The Blue Ridge Mountains of Virginia, North Carolina, South Carolina, Georgia and Tennessee are among the very few places in the world where fairy crosses can be found. However they are quite common in those parts of the United States. Visit Fairy Stone State Park (967 Fairystone Lake Drive, Stuart, VA 24171-9588, phone: (276) 930-2424) for the very best place to hunt for fairy crosses. Park rangers offer complimentary guides on the unique history of the stones. There is also a gift shop with staurolite fairy crosses available for purchase. Staurolite is the official State Mineral of Georgia. The Cherokee County Museum in Murphy, NC also has a good collection of fairy crosses on display (phone: (828) 837-6792). The Smithsonian Institute has several perfect fairy crosses of immense size exhibited in its collection.

—MARINA BRYONY

The Power of the Shadow

THE WORD SHADOW comes from the Old English *sceadu* which itself comes from the Greek *skia thanatou*, a mistranslation of a Hebrew word for "intense darkness." But our version has been added to other words to explain/designate different things. Basically it describes what happens when a solid object interrupts a source of light and causes a darker, blurred copy of its shape to be projected either before or behind what is blocking the light.

But we now use it to describe other things. We speak of "shadowing" a suspect, or describe a medical condition (a shadow on a lung). A shadowed area, or shady place out of the Sun. But it also has a place in the vocabulary of the Mysteries.

Each of us has a "shadow" side to our natures, no matter how good we think we are. The darker shadow side of us is always there waiting for a moment when we hit a point in our lives when we are vulnerable. When some action, thought, event or emotional upset can cause a momentary blocking of the Inner Light and our shadow side comes to the fore. It is then that we can become subject to the darker side of ourself.

We see this in drug addicts, in the overuse of alcohol and in some mental conditions. But it is not only individuals, it can and does happen in gang warfare, in organised crime, in wartime, and seemingly harmless sport meetings. It only needs one or two to take offense at a perceived insult, or a mishap on the playing field for a full-blown riot to erupt into violence. It has been described

"One person or even two or three of you cannot stem the combined shadow power of an entire stadium."

as the **madness of crowds** and is a recognised factor that can take over large gatherings at any time.

Wherever you find an emotionally-charged crowd of people there will always be a potential risk of the shadow side coming to the forefront. Those of us with the knowledge, understanding and training of the Mysteries can often sense the sudden darkening of the crowd mood and know it is time to get out of the vicinity as soon as possible.

You cannot stand against such a force.

One person or even two or three of you cannot stem the combined shadow power of an entire stadium. A small group, yes, with combined effort you might be able to stem the tide, but more than that is not possible.

Often there will be a security force or police who will try, but if you look at TV clips of such happenings you will see how even a reasonably large police group can be overwhelmed. The shadow builds with great speed and feeds off the fear, anger, disappointment and physical energy of thousands of people. You might think of it as a physical/mental/emotional tsunami, and like that phenomenon, it's impossible to halt.

Strangely enough you can get a similar kind of reaction at a large religious meeting. When the emotion builds up and a fervor takes hold of the group mind. This is a different aspect of the shadow. It is not evil or antagonistic, but has a similar effect as it spreads through the crowd, seeking energy and manifesting in healing (though this is usually short-lived) and outbursts of prayer, singing, dancing and religious conversions.

But the shadow is also to be found in all of us, those who follow the old ways learn this in the early days of our training—if we are taught in the right way, and by those who understand the power that lies within all human beings. (Albeit it, often hidden under "civilisation!")

An it harm none

We all know we will meet temptation in our lives, but we guard against our inner shadow knowing that to give in means a backfire reaction to the strength of "Three times Three."

We all know the feeling of wanting to lash out when we are hurt, or when we see injustice happening in front of us, and there are ways in which we can combat it, through law or with other means, *but* to give over the power we have tried so hard to acquire and refine to the Shadow side of us, is to demean it and deprive us of our Inner Light.

Not that you cannot defend, or even at the right time and using the right means *fight back*, but the power and the means must be used with discretion, dignity, and with the understanding that you accept responsibility.

There is such a thing as an "occult police force" to call on. Those who have gone before us, for a time remain with those they love and have taught. That is how they help and that help is *real*.

The shadow side is always there, because we are human, and we still have a lot to learn about being human. One day we will become fully aware of the power we hold within, but until we can use it wisely we will always have to watch for the shadow hiding within. Perhaps you may have been taught when young about having an angel on one shoulder and an imp on the other, both trying to get your attention!

The shadow can be very persuasive, look very inviting, and give you many reasons why you should let it "advise you," but there will always be a cost. The more you let the shadow loose, the harder it is to control. Then the day may come when it becomes the master, not the servant.

—DOLORES ASHCROFT-NOWICKI

Connecting with the Spirits of Place

AN ESSENTIAL PART of Witchcraft is being in tune with not only yourself, but also with the world around you. That knowledge of the world encompasses not only recognizing physical aspects, but also the more liminal ones—the hidden spirits and invisible threads just under the surface.

Many folks hold a deep mental connection to a faraway land where their ancestors came from or perhaps where their spiritual path originated. This is definitely an important connection to keep in mind, but it can be all too easy to overlook the very ground you live on. If you don't take the time to properly familiarize yourself with the land you reside upon, it can be detrimental to your practice. Not only will there be a sense of disjointedness and lack of foundation, but you're also likely to miss out on vital signs of both physical and metaphysical natures.

Even if your path focuses on the lore and seasons of a country halfway across the world, a Witch needs to be rooted where they reside. Look at this as three distinct forms to identify: the building in which you live, the land it sits directly upon, and the ecosystem that the land is a part of. You can keep building layers out from there (neighborhood, city/town, state, region, etc), but begin with orienting yourself first with the closest three spirit kinds.

What are the Spirits of Place?

In ancient times, the *genius loci* (plural *genii locorum*) was said to be the protective spirit of a place. Nowadays, the term has expanded outside the sense of a guardian to the resident spirit of a location. Another term is the numen (plural numina) which is the divine presence found in a place. The spirit of a place can be interpreted as the atmospheric energy or concept of a place, or much more literally as a metaphysical being or

mythic identity. Essentially the Spirit of Place is the identity and conscious energy connected to that location. Whether you're looking at Slavic, Celtic, Icelandic, Italian, Pueblo, or Japanese folklore, you'll find that beings that inhabit wild, sacred, and human-populated spaces all have specific names, characteristics and cultural protocols. So whether you find it easier to connect with specific named beings or more general energy, there is a long history of recognizing the Spirits of Place to draw upon.

Hearth & Home

What is a home? A building is not only a structure that you live and/ or work in—it's the collective sum of all of the materials that it is built from, items placed within it, and the residual effects of everyone and everything that has come through its doors. That includes the beings currently living there, as well as possibly those who have passed on or moved away.

When you move into a new place, walk through the entire space, then take some time to be quiet, listen, and get a sense of how the place feels. Calm? Sad? Anxious? Excited? Before moving things and setting up, physically clean everything, clearing out any dust, dirt, or other debris. If possible, the next thing to do is set up an altar space, generally in the hearth or central area, introducing yourself and your intentions to the space. Next if cleansing is necessary (it's not always), do that, then set up protections on the doors and windows. Regularly, check in on the house and adjust as necessary.

Typically when something feels off or there are physical issues, it's either because the place has gotten messy, neglected, or other people have come through. Opening windows, sweeping the floors, and blessing with incense or an herbal spray are great ways to reconnect and refresh the space. If things go missing or mischief is afoot, leave some offerings to appease or do some sterner workings to clear out unwanted spirits, depending on the feel of things.

Land of Foundation & Focus

The land upon which your home rests is the foundation for everything that happens in and around the dwelling. It is affected not only by the house, but any neighboring structures, street and foot traffic, resident flora and fauna, and the weather. Even if you're surrounded by concrete, there's still earth underneath—and everything moving around and on top of it.

The easiest way to connect with the land is to take care of it, spending time working it. Sweeping and clearing the sidewalks, removing trash that's blown in, planting herbs and flowers, feeding the resident crows, and paying attention to what crosses the yard. It's fascinating to see what plants and animals arrive from year to year—what thrives and what goes missing. If needed, extend wards and protections out from the house to the far corners or designated edges of the property. For some people this means burying crystals or other tokens, and for others it means drawing sigils or planting specific flowers or trees in those spots.

If you have a larger property, you may notice distinct personalities in various areas. Large bushes and trees, streams, and rock formations are likely to have their own sense of spirit. Once again, be still and listen to the feel of these spots, seeing if they are in need of anything. Don't leave or make offerings unless there is a sense that it is the correct and necessary thing to do. Most often, simply being a steward of the Land is exchange enough.

Environment & Landmark Connection

The land that you live on is part of a larger system in many ways: an ecosystem, a neighborhood, a town or city, county, region, etc. If you're having a hard time feeling connected to a place, break out a map and look at what's around you. Make note of the natural characteristics of the land: hills and mountains, streams, lakes, forests, rock formations, old trees, etc. Then look at the human-related landmarks: monuments, historical buildings, sculptures, bridges, parks and other features. These things too have an impact on the feel and flow of things.

Mark what is north, east, south and west of you, and as time allows visit these places and introduce yourself. Take a photo or a respectfully acquired memento (a sample of earth, water, pebble, leaf, flower). Then at home on or near your hearth altar, orient the image or item as it generally sits in relation to where you are. This will help you connect more profoundly with the Spirits of Place, from inside of your home and stretching outward.

The Benefits

Taking the time to be present, listening and being more aware of what's happening directly in your home and the surrounding area will definitely help improve your personal practice. You'll feel more confident as a practitioner, as well as more conscious of everything moving around you. This added awareness will help you to make better and more effective choices on a daily basis. You'll also find the Spirits of Place more likely to aid and work with you, versus the alternative.

—LAURA TEMPEST ZAKROFF

2020 SUNRISE AND SUNSET TIMES

Providence—San Francisco—Sydney—London

	Sunrise				Sunset			
	Prov	**SF**	**Syd**	**Lon**	**Prov**	**SF**	**Syd**	**Lon**
Jan 5	7:14 AM	7:26 AM	5:51 AM	8:06 AM	4:27 PM	5:03 PM	8:08 PM	4:05 PM
15	7:11 AM	7:24 AM	6:00 AM	8:00 AM	4:38 PM	5:13 PM	8:07 PM	4:19 PM
25	7:05 AM	7:19 AM	6:09 AM	7:50 AM	4:50 PM	5:24 PM	8:04 PM	4:35 PM
Feb 5	6:55 AM	7:11 AM	6:20 AM	7:34 AM	5:04 PM	5:36 PM	7:56 PM	4:55 PM
15	6:42 AM	7:00 AM	6:30 AM	7:16 AM	5:17 PM	5:47 PM	7:47 PM	5:13 PM
25	6:28 AM	6:48 AM	6:39 AM	6:56 AM	5:29 PM	5:57 PM	7:36 PM	5:31 PM
Mar 5	6:14 AM	6:35 AM	6:47 AM	6:37 AM	5:40 PM	6:06 PM	7:25 PM	5:47 PM
15	6:57 AM	7:20 AM	6:55 AM	6:14 AM	6:51 PM	7:16 PM	7:12 PM	6:04 PM
25	6:40 AM	7:05 AM	7:03 AM	5:51 AM	7:02 PM	7:25 PM	6:58 PM	6:21 PM
Apr 5	6:21 AM	6:49 AM	6:11 AM	6:27 AM	7:15 PM	7:35 PM	5:43 PM	7:40 PM
15	6:05 AM	6:34 AM	6:18 AM	6:05 AM	7:26 PM	7:44 PM	5:31 PM	7:56 PM
25	5:50 AM	6:21 AM	6:26 AM	5:44 AM	7:37 PM	7:54 PM	5:19 PM	8:13 PM
May 5	5:37 AM	6:09 AM	6:33 AM	5:25 AM	7:47 PM	8:03 PM	5:09 PM	8:29 PM
15	5:26 AM	6:00 AM	6:41 AM	5:09 AM	7:58 PM	8:12 PM	5:01 PM	8:45 PM
25	5:18 AM	5:53 AM	6:48 AM	4:56 AM	8:07 PM	8:20 PM	4:55 PM	8:59 PM
June 5	5:12 AM	5:49 AM	6:54 AM	4:47 AM	8:16 PM	8:27 PM	4:52 PM	9:11 PM
15	5:11 AM	5:48 AM	6:59 AM	4:44 AM	8:21 PM	8:32 PM	4:52 PM	9:18 PM
25	5:13 AM	5:50 AM	7:01 AM	4:45 AM	8:23 PM	8:34 PM	4:54 PM	9:20 PM
July 5	5:18 AM	5:55 AM	7:01 AM	4:52 AM	8:22 PM	8:33 PM	4:58 PM	9:17 PM
15	5:25 AM	6:01 AM	6:58 AM	5:02 AM	8:17 PM	8:29 PM	5:03 PM	9:09 PM
25	5:34 AM	6:09 AM	6:53 AM	5:15 AM	8:09 PM	8:22 PM	5:10 PM	8:57 PM
Aug 5	5:45 AM	6:18 AM	6:44 AM	5:32 AM	7:57 PM	8:12 PM	5:17 PM	8:39 PM
15	5:55 AM	6:26 AM	6:34 AM	5:47 AM	7:43 PM	8:00 PM	5:24 PM	8:20 PM
25	6:05 AM	6:35 AM	6:23 AM	6:03 AM	7:28 PM	7:47 PM	5:31 PM	8:00 PM
Sept 5	6:17 AM	6:44 AM	6:09 AM	6:21 AM	7:10 PM	7:30 PM	5:39 PM	7:35 PM
15	6:27 AM	6:53 AM	5:55 AM	6:37 AM	6:53 PM	7:15 PM	5:45 PM	7:13 PM
25	6:37 AM	7:01 AM	5:41 AM	6:52 AM	6:35 PM	6:59 PM	5:52 PM	6:50 PM
Oct 5	6:48 AM	7:10 AM	6:27 AM	7:09 AM	6:18 PM	6:44 PM	6:59 PM	6:27 PM
15	6:59 AM	7:19 AM	6:14 AM	7:26 AM	6:02 PM	6:30 PM	7:07 PM	6:05 PM
25	7:11 AM	7:29 AM	6:03 AM	6:43 AM	5:47 PM	6:17 PM	7:15 PM	4:45 PM
Nov 5	6:24 AM	6:40 AM	5:52 AM	7:02 AM	4:33 PM	5:05 PM	7:25 PM	4:24 PM
15	6:36 AM	6:51 AM	5:44 AM	7:19 AM	4:23 PM	4:57 PM	7:35 PM	4:09 PM
25	6:48 AM	7:01 AM	5:39 AM	7:36 AM	4:17 PM	4:51 PM	7:44 PM	3:58 PM
Dec 5	6:58 AM	7:11 AM	5:38 AM	7:50 AM	4:14 PM	4:49 PM	7:53 PM	3:52 PM
15	7:07 AM	7:19 AM	5:39 AM	8:00 AM	4:14 PM	4:51 PM	8:01 PM	3:50 PM
25	7:12 AM	7:24 AM	5:44 AM	8:06 AM	4:19 PM	4:56 PM	8:06 PM	3:55 PM

Prov=Providence; SF=San Francisco; Syd=Sydney; Lon=London
Times are presented in the standard time of the geographical location, using the current time zone of that place.

Window on the Weather

Since the dawn of time, humankind has pursued the knowledge of things to come with vehemence only matched by the species' will to survive and perpetuate in its time on this green Earth. The pursuit to know the right time to conceive, marry, conquer, travel and sow has been over-riding. Some of the methods employed in these very important pursuits have been esoteric, as well as scientific. Our need to discern future weather conditions has not been exempt from our need to know.

The prediction of weather has moved from the domain of the priest-seer to the domain of the meteorological scientist, relying on the review of past data and multiple variables in the present in order to glimpse conditions of the future. While looking into the weather for tomorrow or next week can be a laborious task, forecasting a year can be wrought with intricacies that are complex beyond the imagination.

Meteorologists use many tools to tackle long-term weather forecasting. In creating this *Window on the Weather*, our meteorologist Tom Lang considers orientation of the Earth in its orbit, the irregular shape of orbit, cosmic disturbances such as Sun spots, interstellar radiation and human activity, along with a myriad of other variables that will influence trends for 2020..

SPRING

MARCH 2020 Early spring is often an active time for tornadoes from the Gulf Coast to Florida. Still near the solar minimum, activity is likely to be somewhat subdued. There will however be a sharp boundary between lingering arctic cold across the Ohio valley, Great Lakes and Southeast U.S., with warmth setting the stage for excessive rainfall from Georgia through the Carolinas. The recent trend of late winter snow is likely to occur again, focused from New England west to the Great Lakes. The coldest air nationally will be concentrated across the Northern Plains with occasional incursions into the Pacific Northwest southward in California, where heavy mountain snows are likely once more. Temperatures in Texas show greater variance than normal, and a tornado swarm may strike Oklahoma.

APRIL 2020 Cool east winds persist along the East Coast, a signature of low cloud cover induced at low solar cycle cosmic particles. Spring will be slow to arrive there and west-bound through the Great Lakes, where extensive ice coverage will be slow to melt. Spring snows are heavy throughout the Rockies and Sierra Nevada. Paradoxically, heavy spring rainfall will set the stage for an aggressive fire season as extensive undergrowth will dry and become combustible later in the summer and fall. April brings the peak of the tornado season to the southeast, though available energy for such storms has diminished, reducing the threat somewhat. Rainfall remains heavy across the Mississippi and Ohio Valleys.

MAY 2020 Summer heat arrives early from Georgia through Florida and west to Texas. That pattern is "antecedent" or a "dipole" to conditions in the Pacific Northwest that are cool and damp. Such contrasts are common across the planet and part of an alternating current system of natural checks and balances. Such land-based heat dispersion originates in the planet's oceans where contrasting pools of warm and cool water define the jet stream and subsequent global airflow. Furthermore, submerged volcanic activity sends plumes of water vapor poleward and regulates night-time temperatures globally and arctic circle snowfall during late spring.

SUMMER

JUNE 2020 The Summer Solstice arrives with limited heat nationally. A late frost is possible across the Dakotas and Montana. Otherwise, growing conditions should be ideal for farmers. A weak la Niña may develop which lends support for an early season tropical storm close to the Gulf Coast. Otherwise, the primary focus of heat will be from the Carolinas to Florida. The Ohio Valley and Plains turn drier, and limited short-term drought conditions may emerge in Texas. Passing cold fronts bring the risk for severe weather several times in New England. Cool and misty weather extend from Seattle to Portland. Dry weather expands farther south in California.

JULY 2020 In any year, the annual peak in summer heat occurs on average about three weeks past the Solstice. This occurs as the balance between solar radiation input and outgoing warmth as night lags the actual date of maximum solar input. Rates of solar absorption are determined by the planet's various material compositions and colors. The latter regulates rates of solar reflection. This summer is likely to be hotter than normal from the northern plains to the southeast U.S. However, low solar input and moderate humidity levels will limit the extent of the heat and bring pleasant night time temperatures. Intrusions of cool air will be common in the Northeast and Pacific Northwest. The fire season begins in California.

AUGUST 2020 Common during la Niña "ENSO" events, the hurricane season is likely to be somewhat more aggressive than in recent years. Along with an increase in the number of storms, with high pressure strong across the continent, the wind fields associated with this year's storms will remain strong as many hurricanes reach the shoreline. At risk; The Gulf Coast and Southeast U.S., along with parts of the southern and central East Coast. In general, rainfall will be light across much of the nation, though a monsoon flow will become established along the Appalachians. The fire danger continues to increase in California, a consequence of widespread undergrowth from previous winter rainfall.

AUTUMN

SEPTEMBER 2020 September 10th is the peak of the hurricane season across the Atlantic Basin. While the number of hurricanes is likely to be elevated this year, with low ultraviolet solar radiation and somewhat cooler Atlantic Ocean water temperatures, activity will still be somewhat curtailed compared to previous decades. Of great concern is the fire danger across the west coast. The ongoing la Niña favors low humidity along previously mentioned enhanced undergrowth. The harvest is underway with warmer than normal temperatures favored for the nation's midsection. The ongoing pattern globally favors two months of above normal temperatures followed by equal and opposite conditions for a similar duration.

OCTOBER 2020 Hurricane frequency eases in the Atlantic and temperatures remain relatively warm across the United States. Rainfall is generally sparse, supportive of the nation's economy. The big concern remains West Coast fires as pressure systems this month favor strong winds across southern California. With dry weather nationally, nighttime temperatures turn cool quickly and the first frosts become likely in locations such as Western Montana, Northern Minnesota, Michigan and interior valleys of Northern New England. Florida remains hotter than normal with daytime highs in the 90s. Texas also remains unusually hot and dry.

NOVEMBER 2020 Following the Sun, mammals' endocrine and limbic systems that regulate fertility and other behaviors, respond to changes in solar ultraviolet radiation output. A sudden drop during fall is a signal to hibernate as cold weather usually follows in about four days. Such a solar drop also shortens jet stream wavelengths and allows gathering cold air at high latitudes to plunge south suddenly. That is the likely scenario this year, still near the 11-year solar minimum, during which that dynamic is most pronounced. Snows will likely arrive early in the mountains, even as California fires persist. The turn to cold weather will be most prevalent along the East Coast and intense heat will end in Florida.

WINTER

DECEMBER 2020 Below-normal temperatures and earlier than normal snowfall can be expected this year with the chances for a white Yule above average, about 50% in Boston and 30% in New York. Lake effect snows occur across western New York, Ohio and Michigan. In general, surges of arctic air will spread from the Northern Plains across the eastern two thirds of the nation. Such a positioning of the cold will lead to December snows in Denver with ski areas enjoying fine conditions. Eastern Seaboard snow occurrences will arrive with so called "Alberta Clippers," though late in the month, a storm may arrive from the Gulf of Mexico with heavier snowfall.

JANUARY 2021 January is likely to be brutally cold across much of the nation with the threat of freezing temperatures as far south as central Florida. Travel trouble persists near the Great Lakes as arctic air induces local blizzard conditions there. Rochester, NY, Grand Rapids and the eastern Suburbs of Cleveland are especially vulnerable. Interestingly, this pattern also supports snowfall for parts of the Pacific Northwest; not just cities such as Spokane but even Seattle may see some snow action. California remains dry and vulnerable to fire. Several "blue northers" sweep through Oklahoma and Texas with the chances for at least a brief snowfall as far south as Houston. Boston and New York City have 150% of normal snowfall, in addition to below-normal temperatures.

FEBRUARY 2021 The worst of the bitter cold will ease early in the month but with some tradeoffs. The sudden return of mild weather will be accompanied by a brief, fierce snowfall along the I95 corridor and briefly shutting down cities from Washington to Portland, Maine. However, such conditions will be transient as a major thaw begins before the tenth and lasts much of the month for areas east of the Rockies. At last, the fire danger eases in California as the jet stream relocates farther west and allows storms to bring wet weather where it is badly needed. Mountain snows will be heavy too, promising abundant water supplies by summer. Denver receives more snow and inter-mountain travel remains hazardous at times.

LES DOMINOS

DOMINO DIVINATION

MANY GAMES of chance are also methods of divination. Dice and cards are among the most well-known examples, but dominoes were also used to tell fortunes and glimpse the future. As recently as the middle years of the twentieth century, domino divination was commonly practiced in North America. It went out of fashion with the late twentieth century explosion of interest in tarot cards and astrology, but the rules can still be found in old books, and it makes a lively and interesting oracle.

To practice domino divination, you'll need an ordinary set of dominoes. If you haven't played dominoes before, the usual set contains 28 wooden tiles. Each tile is divided into two squares, and each square has between zero and six dots on it, arranged like the pips on dice. Before you cast a reading, place all the dominoes on a table or other flat surface, with the dotted sides down, and mix them up thoroughly by sweeping them around with your hands.

Once the dominoes are thoroughly mixed, decide on the question you want to ask and then begin the reading. If you want to use the traditional method, close your eyes and put a finger down onto a domino. Take that one out from among the others, turn it over, and interpret it. Then put it back in, mix the dominoes up again, and repeat the process. According to old books, a maximum of three dominoes should be read for one person at one sitting, and it's unlucky to read dominoes for any one person more than once a month. Another traditional rule holds that it's unlucky to read dominoes for anyone on a Monday or a Friday, though some of the old guides to domino divination dispute this.

Note that it doesn't matter which way the dominoes are oriented when you read them. If you draw a Three-Two, for example—that is, a domino with three dots in one square and two dots in the other—it reads the same whether the three or the two is further away from you.

These are the meanings of the dominoes:

Double-Blank: This domino is considered the worst of all, as it brings disappointment and loss to everyone except those who gain by deception, cheating and fraud. For them, it is an excellent sign, and means they will be able to keep what they gain. Other people will find it a bad sign for business as well

as in love. It may mean loss of money or possessions, or even loss of a job.

Double-Ace: This is a symbol of happiness. It is favorable for love and friendship, promising harmony and affection between the people involved, and it also indicates financial gain and economic security.

Two-Blank: Dishonesty and misfortune in most things are indicated by this domino. If the question concerns a relationship, whether a love affair or a business partnership, the other partner is cheating. On the other hand, if the question concerns travel, the indications are excellent, predicting a pleasant and safe journey.

Two-One: This domino indicates wealth and comfort, but it can also lead to extravagance. In questions having to do with relationships, it is neither good nor ill, and suggests that the benefits of the relationship are balanced neatly against the disadvantages. In all questions having to do with money, it warns of carelessness and excessive expenditure. Guard against an unbalanced budget.

Double-Two: Thrift and prudence lead to success in business and a happy home life. Prosperity and happiness in the future as a result of self-restraint and careful management today.

Three-Blank: An indication of quarrels. Do not enter into the relationship you are considering; the

two of you will argue. If you are going to a social gathering, be careful to avoid getting in an argument or talking about any controversial subject.

Three-One: Scandal, unhappiness and embarrassment. Be careful to avoid any dishonorable action or underhanded dealing. You will be caught, and there is a danger of lawsuits or criminal charges should the situation justify it.

Three-Two: A lucky combination for relationships and business alike. You will succeed at anything you try. It is particularly fortunate for traveling. Special care should be given to children at this time, however, or they will feel neglected.

Double-Three: This is a sign of money on its way to you. Substantial sums of money and general abundance are indicated by this domino.

Four-Blank: Disappointments are in store, for promises that have been made to you will not be kept. If you have a secret, do not reveal it to anyone, for they will spread it around. If the client is a pregnant woman, this domino suggests that she will have twins or even triplets.

Four-One : An indication of gradual improvement. Things will get better a little at a time. Great happiness and success in due time. Prosperity is on its way.

Four-Two: Change is coming, for good or ill. A time of happiness will give way to unhappiness, and vice versa; a lover may have a change of heart, or someone who has refused you may decide to reconsider. Business that has been slow will improve. Nothing will stay the same when this domino is drawn.

Four-Three : Play it safe, aim for what you know you can achieve, and you will prosper, augurs this domino. There are risks but you can avoid them with prudence, patience and modest ambitions.

Double-Four : This domino promises prosperity for craftspeople and all those who work with their hands. For others, it warns that patience will be required and much time may pass before expected benefits arrive. On the other hand, it indicates pleasant social interactions and a time for fun and relaxation. It can predict a wedding.

Five-Blank: This domino warns of deception and self-deception. In love, business, and all other affairs of life, beware of false pretenses and promises that will not be kept. Accept no propositions, sign no contracts, and begin no projects under this influence, for you will lose whatever is at stake.

Five-One: Bad for money, this domino predicts financial disappointment, but it is favorable for friendships and social interactions and predicts a busy, happy, but potentially expensive time.

Five-Two: Haste is unfortunate when this domino appears, and new ventures of all kinds should be put on hold for the time being. Patience, tolerance, and prudence are called for, in order to avoid making a mistake that will take a long time to mend. Avoid

lasting commitments of all kinds and investigate everything thoroughly.

Five-Three: This domino portends calm and stability, a period in which slow improvement can take place but no sudden changes can be expected. Do not expect to gain much during this time. Instead, concentrate on laying foundations for gain hereafter, or simply enjoy a period of relative peace and comfort.

Five-Four: Headstrong, willful behavior is predicted by this domino, and the results will not be good. Hopes and wishes will be disappointed, and others may take advantage of your unwise actions. This domino is also unfavorable for all financial affairs; it threatens loss of money, and in particular warns that investments will not live up to their promise.

Double-Five: This domino, by contrast, indicates great success in every department of life. It promises great things to those with initiative and enterprise, and predicts plenty of money and the achievement of your goals.

Six-Blank: This is an unhappy sign, and it signifies financial difficulties and bad news. A family member or someone else of importance to you may be ill, or in trouble.

Six-One: This domino predicts a mixture of successes and troubles. It often means difficulties at the beginning but success later on. Continued effort is called for, since first attempts may fail but later efforts succeed. Be prepared for the long haul.

Six-Two: A lucky domino for all those who are honest and fair in their

dealings with others, it threatens serious trouble for the dishonest and the unfair. Secrets will be revealed, for good or ill, and the truth will be found out.

Six-Three: The most fortunate draw for lovers, promising a happy and enduring relationship, this domino is also a good sign for all other questions. It is favorable for wealth and for success in one's career.

Six-Four: This domino is one of calm and contentment, promising smooth sailing in love, business and life in general.

Six-Five: Perseverance is the watchword for this domino. In questions concerning business and career, you may have to start over somewhere else. If investments are at issue, your chances of seeing any return are minimal. If poor health is the trouble, accept your burden for the time being and seek healing. If disappointed in love, there is someone else much more worthy of your affection and devotion. Be sure of every detail before you commit to anything.

Double-Six: This is the domino of improbable good luck. Speculative investments pay off handsomely, blind dates lead to happy long-term relationships, job interviews land a position much better than expected. Take a chance and shoot for the Moon, and you may achieve much more than you expect.

—JOHN MICHAEL GREER

EMBODYING A GOD-FORM

WETHER YOU WORK in the Craft or Ceremonial Magic sooner or later you will find it necessary to "assume" a God-form, or even an angelic form. But God or Angel building, assuming and then using another "Form" is not the easiest thing in the world. It may seem so.

"I'll just think about being Apollo or Demeter and speak the words..." does not cut it. All that does is 1) give you a completely false idea of the God/dess or 2) allows you to simply be YOU in fancy dress, or 3) if you really screw up several days of not being able to find "your real self."

There is an art to embodying God-forms, and dressing up in a transparent robe and carrying a sheaf of corn or wearing a golden loincloth and Sun-ray crown does not bring through much in the way of power. The Form must be built up in the right way so it can and will affect the ritual itself. It needs four things considered:

1. How the form is built and taken on all levels.
2. How much power goes into the form.
3. What *kind* of power and how it is to be used.
4. How the residue of that power is dispersed.

The first rule is simple: get to know your God-form. Look at sculptures and pictures and get an idea of the form, clothing—even footwear—style of hair and their usual posture. How do they stand or hold themselves. In front of a mirror try out these things and slowly build an inner picture of the form in your mind, *but* with your face.

Meditate on the myths associated with the deity, what symbols they carry or use.

Think of a small statue of the form resting in the solar plexus, the place of energy and power, and allow the energy of the God to find a place there. But keep it small, don't let it grow too big or the power may be too much to hold comfortably. Its like a key to a treasure box, when you need to embody that form in ritual you simply recall the small statue in the solar plexus.

(By the way, some God-forms will not suit you or fit well with your own persona. If this is the case, don't push things.)

None of this work is lost. It's not just in ritual that it can be used, but can be called forth in certain circumstances in real life when you need that kind of power or authority. In ritual there are several ways in which the form can be called forth.

1. The statue can be increased in size slowly and carefully until it fits over your own form, then allow the power to fill you up.
2. You can associate a color with the form, and see it as a colored mist that covers you imparting power as it does so.
3. You can see it behind you as a shadow that moves over you, and covers you with itself.

You can work with 2 or 3 different forms so you can use them in different rituals. Think of them as special clothing hanging in a mental wardrobe ready for use.

Craft and Ceremonial are not the only source of such imagery. Some rituals use angelic forms. These need

slightly different ways of building and usage. God-Forms are creations of the created, to use one of Ernest Butlers descriptions. Meaning that human minds have given them form and changed them through the ages. Angelics are formed from much finer articles of energy and can be harder to handle.

The difference is that with a God-form the energy slowly releases into the ritual itself. With angelics that energy is retained in the human form and takes longer to fade. This can be very tiring and also leaves a kind of euphoria that tends to hang around for a while.

Again study the angel full before calling it into yourself. Its power, symbols, attributes, clothing, color (angelics respond to color very strongly). They are usually associated with a direction as well, its hard to call on Michael (Fire) when you are in the West (Water). Also angelics are not easy to handle, their power comes direct from the centre of the Universe. God Forms are less fine and more earthed.

With practice you can build up a selection of such images and their particular power. Always begin to build up the image at least 30 to 60 minutes before ritual—that gives *your* persona and physical body time to prepare—especially with angelics. Decrease the power and form slowly at the end and *please* always *offer* a blessing in exchange.

In many ways all this is done in the same way that an actor builds up a character in a play. In fact a good actor is really an accomplished magician and can "become" someone very different for a space of time. Plus, theatre came out of ritual in the first place.

Taking on a God-form of either gender or in any tradition needs skill and attention to detail. More than ever in ritual, the effect can be either electrifying or a real bore. Also what is being used can suddenly become twice the power imagined and wreck you to your core. Don't panic, allow the presence full reign—it will not harm you. You might have a really bad headache, but physically and spiritually you won't be harmed, unless you have called up something from the dark side.

Learning to "house" a God-form or angelic offers a taste of a very different kind of power and one that takes getting used to. But it can enhance a ritual to the point of exaltation.

Humanity does it all the time without knowing it. When a girl gives you that "come on over" look, she is unknowingly housing Aphrodite. Same goes for the guys, they are being Apollo.

—DOLORES ASHCROFT-NOWICKI

 HOLEY STONES

STONES WITH A HOLE in the center have been used to see the future for centuries. *The Mabinogion*, whose stories were compiled in Middle Welsh in the 12th–13th centuries from oral traditions of the past, mentions a stone given to Peredur that allows him to see and additionally kill an invisible creature. Pliny the Elder, who finished writing his *Natural History* in 77 CE, refers to adder stones, believed to have been made from the hardened saliva of a mass of serpents writhing together whose tongues make up the perforation (hole) in the middle.

A more recent accounting of the power of holed or holey stones comes from the 17th century. Call him the Brahan Seer, Warlock of the Glen, the Scottish Nostradamus or Coinneach Odhar, this Scot was known for his prognostications. Known throughout all the north country for his acquaintance with the unseen world, the Brahan Seer was feared, yet was frequently requested for his services as a Witch, wizard and necromancer.

One such client was Lady Seaforth, wife of the Earl of Seaforth. Her husband had traveled to Paris on some alleged commercial venture, leaving her behind at Brahan Castle. When his stay exceeded the original estimate and the Countess had no letters for several months, she became worried. This was the time before global news broadcasts, telephones or—ye gods, text messages!—and she had no way to determine what had happened. Had he needed to stay longer, but his message had been lost? Had some horrible uprising happened at court during his visit? Had he been waylaid upon the journey home?

With no other recourse, she dispatched messengers to Strathpeffer to summon the Brahan Seer. When brought before the Countess and informed of his task, he asked a few questions about where Lord Seaforth was thought to be

and confirmed that if his lordship was still alive, he should be able to find him.

He drew out his usual instrument of divination, a round white stone with a naturally occurring hole in the middle. Looking through the hole, the seer laughed. "Fear not for your lord. He is safe and sound, well and hearty, merry and happy!" The worried Countess wanted to know more. Where was he? Who was he with? Was he coming home soon? The seer tried to dissuade her from asking more. "Be satisfied. Ask no questions. Let it suffice you to know that your lord is well and merry."

She wasn't satisfied with his vague statements. She pressed on, offering bribes and then even making threats. Eventually he told her the dismal truth.

"My lord seems to have little thought of you or of his children or of his Highland home. I see him in a gay, gilded room, grandly decked out in velvets and silks and cloth of gold and on his knees before a fair lady, her hand pressed to his lips!"

You know the old saying, "Don't shoot the messenger?" The Countess didn't. Instead, she had him hanged for disclosing this embarrassment in the presence of some of the principal retainers of the house of Seaforth, besmirching the good name of both her husband and herself.

Before he was executed, he had one last prognostication to make.

"The long-descended line of Seaforth will, ere many generations have passed, end in extinction and in sorrow. I see a Chief, the last of his house, both deaf and dumb. He will

be the father of three fair sons, all of whom he will follow to the tomb. He will live care-worn and die mourning, knowing that the honours of his line are to be extinguished forever and that no future Chief of the Mackenzies shall bear rule at Brahan or in Kintail. After lamenting over the last and most promising of his sons, he himself shall sink into the grave and the remnant of his possessions shall be inherited by a lassie from the East, with snow in her bonnet. She is to kill her sister and as a sign by which it may be known that these things are coming to pass, there shall be four great lairds in the days of the last deaf and dumb Seaforth, viz., Gairloch, Chisholm, Grant and Rasay, of whom one shall be buck-toothed, another hair-lipped, another half-witted and the fourth a stammerer."

Did the Brahan Seer's prophecy come true? According to The Vicissitudes of Families by Sir Bernard Burke, published in 1869, it seems they did.

How He Found the Stone

One legend says that one day the Brahan Seer was napping on what turned out to be a fairy hill. Upon awakening, he found a small stone in his pocket which allowed him to see the future by looking through the hole in its middle.

Yet another legend involves his mother. One evening, while she was tending her cattle on the side of a ridge called Cnoceothail, overlooking the burying-ground of Baile-na-Cille, in Uig, she saw all the graves in the churchyard opening. A multitude of ghosts rose up and left, returning in about an hour's time. She noticed that one grave near the side was still open. Curious and abnormally brave, she went to the grave and placed her "cuigeal" (distaff) in it, for it was said that the occupant could not enter the grave while a cuigeal rested in it.

Soon a spirit came rushing toward her, entreating her "Lift thy distaff from off my grave and let me enter my dwelling of the dead." The mother agreed she would do so only if the spirit told her what detained her. The ghost replied that she was a daughter of the King of Norway who went to visit her land, which, being far away, took her longer than the rest.

If, the spirit promised, the woman would remove her distaff, she would reward her. "Go and find in yonder lake a small round blue stone, which give to your son, who by it shall reveal future events."

The woman did as requested and gave the stone to her son. No sooner had she done this than he was endowed with the gift of divination and his fame spread far and wide.

Finding Your Stone

Unlike Pliny's adder stones, regular holed stones are relatively easy to find. The modern belief is that any stone with a hole bored through the middle naturally by water can be used for divination. That is, it must be bored by the action of the sea or a river; creating one with a high-pressure water hose will not create an instrument of divination.

So the next time you're near water, look for stones. I've been unable to find any on the Atlantic coastline of New England, but I did find quite a few on the shoreline in Tel Aviv, Israel. Just keep looking.

—MORVEN WESTFIELD

Hekate and the Twin Torches

SHE WHO RULES the earth, the seas and the heavens...her powers know no limits. They have no boundaries. Hekate is often seen with tools; and in her triple form, She has six hands with which to wield them. One should not forget—She requires no tools to get the job done. So, it is important to remember that the tools are symbols. And in symbol, there is meaning.

So what does it mean when She appears in human form, with two hands, and in each there is a torch?

Consider this: a single tool in both hands implies dedication to a single purpose; or if you prefer,

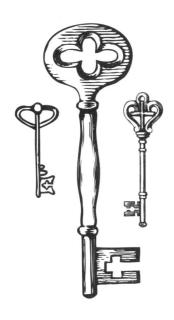

representation of a single aspect. Hekate with the twin torches is Phosphoros—Light-Bringer.

Light-Bringers are predominately solar deities. In Greco-Roman and even Persian cultures, the most powerful solar deities were male. Sun gods were often jealous gods. In his heyday as a mighty Titan, Hyperion/Helios was no exception to that rule—guarding the powers of the Sun and wielding that power at will, whether for creation or destruction. His light shone so brightly that it would blind your eyes with a glance, or devour you completely if you dared creep too close.

Hekate, on the other hand, consumes the power of the Sun; and with her receptive nature, She transforms it. Magicians, occultists and witches alike have a common understanding of polarity, the unifying principal of apparent opposites, which when brought together in balance create a whole greater than the sum of its parts: positive and negative, male and female, force and form, light and darkness, outward and inward, et cetera. When Hekate bears the powers of the Sun, they are filtered through the divine feminine.

As an NECTW Priestess and a devotee of Hekate, I feel compelled to share the following:

As Propolos, Hekate carried the light in her hands and led Persephone from the Underworld. As Dadouchos, She chooses to walk among us carrying that light, holding it out before us, and leading us through the darkness. Hekate the Light-Bringer has brought me comfort—I no longer fear the darkness. Hekate the torch-bearer has illuminated the shadows on my path and within myself. There will always be darkness and light, yet darkness illuminated by the light of a sacred torch reveals mysteries beyond our ability to imagine them.

Embrace the whole and become greater than the sum of its parts. Hekate, bearer of the twin torches, stands ready to guide you.

—SPARROW

The Hardanger Fiddle

THE VIOLIN OR FIDDLE has held a prominent place in the folk music of many countries for hundreds of years. Its transportability and ability to encapsulate a myriad of styles and nuances has provided a varied and sophisticated palette for the folk musician to work with.

Whilst the violin is a commonly recognised instrument worldwide, the Hardanger fiddle (or Hardingfele) is less well known outside of its native Norway, specifically the northwestern area of the country.

The oldest example of a Hardanger fiddle comes from 1651, made by Ole Jonsen Jaastad who was from the western district of Hardanger. It appears far more elaborately decorated than the violin and often has an intricately carved scroll depicting an animal or a woman's head. The fingerboards of the Hardanger fiddle are equally as decorative and are often inlaid with mother of pearl or occasionally bone.

The Hardanger has had a mixed and often turbulent relationship with the Christian Church. Initially the early instrument makers benefited from learning parts of their craft such as the carving and varnishing of the instrument from preachers and lay ministers, but over time the instrument became associated with the Devil (or the *Nix*, shapeshifting female water creatures of Norwegian culture) and church members to declared "that it would be best for the soul if the fiddles be burned."

The Hardanger fiddle, unlike the violin, has eight strings, four of which are played and four which sit underneath the bridge and resonate sympathetically with the string being bowed. There are more than 20 different tunings for these strings which are dependent on the region in which the melody being performed comes from. One such tuning from the Valdres area of Norway is called the "Troll" tuning and is used specifically for a melody called *fanitullen*, the Devil's tunes. The fanitullen melody is believed to have been composed during a bloody and violent wedding which took place on a farm in the village of Hol in Hallingdal during 1724. When one of the guests went to get more mead during the event, he reported seeing the Devil himself sat upon a barrel, playing the melody on his fiddle. For "troll tuning" the Hardanger's played strings are tuned to the notes A E A C# , the notes which form the A major triad in western classical music whilst the sympathetic strings are tuned C# E C# A. This tuning limits the overall range of the fiddle so is not commonly used but it is known by several other names in different regions of Norway such as *huldrestille* in Seljord, perhaps referencing its ties to the *huldra*, and is also known as *grålysingstille* in Valdres, the name for the first light in the sky before dawn breaks.

Troll tuning is used for melodies from the Kivlemøyane suite which tells the tale of three maids who were bell ringers for a Catholic church during mass. Their music was said to be so enchanting that it distracted the congregation who left to listen to the music from outside. Enraged, the priest cursed the three maids, turning them to stone. Their image can be seen in a stone formation of a valley in Kivledalen. Similar tales relating to women turning to stone appear around the world such as Stanton Drew stone circles in Somerset. In another area of the UK, Mitchell's Fold stone circle has a similar tale to tell where one of the stones belonging to the circle is believed to be a Witch who tried to milk a magical cow which had appeared during a famine. Images of the story are found carved into the pews and pillars of the local church, placed there by the parish priest.

—JERA

For a clip of music with a hardanger fiddle visit us at TheWitchesAlmanac. com/almanac-extras/

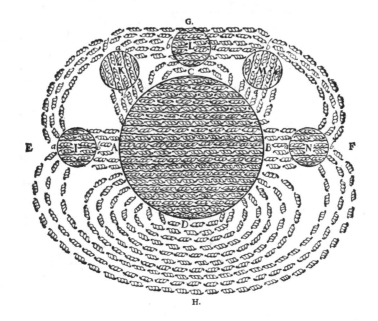

LODESTONES

"The corner-stone of MAGIC is an intimate practical knowledge of magnetism and electricity, their qualities, correlations and potencies... There are occult properties in many other minerals, equally strange with that in the lodestone, which all practitioners of magic must know and of which so-called exact science is wholly ignorant."

—H. P. Blavatsky, *Isis Unveiled*

One of only a few minerals found naturally magnetized, Lodestone is a piece of magnetite, an oxide of iron suspected to becomes magnetized when lightning strikes the ground nearby. The strong electrical field surrounding the lightning rearranges its magnetic domain. The fact that lodestones are mostly found near the Earth's surface where lightning has struck supports this theory.

Iron is usually associated with the planet Mars and therefore so is lodestone. It has also been associated with Saturn, probably because of its color, which is black to a slivery gray. Others associate it with Mercury, again probably due to the color. This inconsistency is not usually a problem in ritual and other magical uses, since the focus is on the magnetism, not planetary associations. After all, it was seeing two stones cling together or move toward each other on their own that alerted the ancients to the potential uses of these stones.

What's in a Name
One legend states that magnetite got its name from a Greek shepherd

named Magnes who became aware of it when small black stones clung to the nails in his sandals. Others believe that the stone was named after the Magnesia region of Thessaly, where it was found. Magnesia, the home of the Magnetes tribe, was an important center of iron production.

In Middle English, lodestone means "course stone" or "leading stone," "lode" being the word for "journey." The earliest uses of lodestones were as compasses. Pieces of lodestone were suspended from a cord or string so they could turn to indicate the way. Another method was to magnetize an iron needle by stroking it several times in a single direction across the lodestone, then inserting the needle in a piece of straw and floating it in a bowl of water where the needle would indicate north and south.

Uses in Magic

It's not surprising that early humans found magnetism in action incomprehensible. How did a piece of rock move? Was there a living being inside? What made the attraction so strong? The Romans believed that the lodestone recruited its strength from iron.

It's not surprising that occasionally those who found this rare mineral used it to their advantage. It is said that Roman priests, aiming to impress their followers, set a small image of Venus made from lodestone close to an image of Mars made of iron, then watched the audience's astonishment as the statues moved toward each other.

The Roman poet Claudian mentioned a similar setup used during marriage ceremonies. The participants believed the attracting powers of the lodestone kept husband and wife together. Lodestones were often set in wedding rings for this purpose.

Uses in Hoodoo

Lodestones can be used magickally to attract anything, but they are most commonly used for love or abundance. Large stones are used for prosperity and luck that you want to continually bring in. They can also be used for other personal spellwork.

Smaller stones pull their power from a large stone. Male and female ones, distinguished by their shape, are used for amatory attraction and to keep lovers together. A male stone has a cylindrical, phallic shape, whereas a female stone may be more triangular. Van Van oil is commonly used to anoint these stones. Small ones may also be used when doing spellwork for others (for example, in drawing away pain from the body) and are returned to the Earth after use. For personal spellwork, place them in a pouch or mojo bag and carry it with you.

After obtaining a lodestone, practitioners commonly give it a name before working with it. After telling the stone its name, the practitioner gives it instructions about its purpose. A naming for a personal stone might go like this:

"I name thee [Name] and ask that you bring me prosperity and luck…"

Stones used for attracting couples are given the names of the people they represent and placed apart. Gradually they are moved closer together as the practitioner describes how their attraction is growing. The stones are moved each day until they finally stick together. If the spell is to just reinforce a love bond (say, for example, on the anniversary of a handfasting or marriage), they can be placed together from the beginning and be instructed to remain fast and true.

Caring for your Lodestone

In the hoodoo/conjure/rootwork tradition, lodestones are considered living beings. Some believe the lightning strike that magnetizes them breathes life into them.

Clean lodestones with whiskey or alcohol-based colognes such as Hoyt's Cologne, Florida Water or Kananga Water. In 1930, Sir E. A. Wallis Budge, in *Amulets and Talismans*, said to place it "in water on Friday so that it may drink" and then lay it in the Sun, but the water bath is discouraged these days. Water can rust the lodestone. Also, as living beings, they must be treated with respect and leaving a lodestone soaking in water — some rootworkers feel — is disrespectful. Instead, use whiskey. Pour, drop or mouth-spray

whiskey on the stone as you thank it for what it has brought you.

To feed them, sprinkle a bit of iron fillings or magnetic sand on them periodically. Some do this every day, but others do it weekly. If the lodestone becomes overloaded with magnetic sand, dust it off and keep it in a container for reuse.

Keep them away from heat, which can damage or completely ruin the lodestone. A hard fall from a high place can also affect the magnetization, so be careful not to drop them. Don't leave them out in a place where people might be tempted to handle them, which disturbs the energy. Don't store them in magnetized containers, which, it is believed, drains the magnetism from the stone. Instead, use a wooden, glass or non-ferrous metal.

Talk to your lodestone at least daily. Remind it of your need. Thank it for what it has already brought you. If you feed them and take care of them, they will attract what you desire.

−NEVROM YDAL

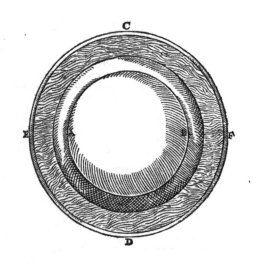

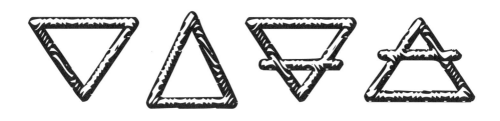

Nature's Secret Magic

WITCH. WICCE. WISE ONE. Seer of the Sacred. The etymology of "witch" lies rooted 5500 years ago in the Proto-Indo-European wicce, bearing fruit as the shamanism of our indigenous ancestors. But lots of Witches have another definition: a Witch is a bender of unseen forces. Witches of all sorts talk about "magick with a k" as Aleister Crowley's: "Science and Art of causing Change to occur in conformity with Will," gentled slightly by Dion Fortune's: "Magick is the art of causing changes in consciousness in conformity with the Will," also directed to affect the outcome of events.

Witches of many persuasions talk about "summoning" and "using" the elements, projecting their willpower and "manipulating" energy to manifest their magic(k). They declare that energy is neutral like electricity, to be used as one chooses. The Rede guides the choices but it's a low moral bar of benign selfishness—do whatever you want, just don't do any harm requiring enforcement by the Threefold Law, threatening punishment that triples whatever harm you do.

Though calling Nature sacred, many Witches still make magic as if Creation is an inanimate machine operated with quantum magic, like a mechanic making a magical car run in an alternate, akashic reality. Drive as fast as you want, wherever you want, just don't run anyone over. But mechanical magic is like trying to drive a car with a fuel of ego, gratification and willpower. Like relying on the carbon fuels wrecking Mother Earth, ultimately, you aren't going anywhere because you'll have nowhere to go.

So how do we make magic, with or without a k? Let's start with those unseen forces we've been attempting to bend. For all of our glorious rebellion, Witches are creatures of our culture, living with the same blindfold everyone wears, a blindfold tied on by history and habit, a blindfold that leaves us unable to see the Sacred. It was tied on long ago, when some of our ancestors thrust divinity into a distant heaven, so far away that God, always male and served by male officiants, disappeared into transcendent realms and abstract thought.

Dogma declared Spirit separate from the world, except for rare, always male, prophetic incarnations. Creation was deemed inanimate, animals soulless, plants irrelevant and humans fallen from grace, though God granted us dominion over Nature for our own selfish purposes. Science and technology, capitalism and consumerism, all devoid of any sense of the numinous, are the heirs to our separation from the Sacred. That illusion is our blindfold.

What's the difference between Witches bending unseen forces to their will with spells and magic and bending Nature to our will with science and technology? Both entitlements stem from the same myth of separation and superiority, the same mania of domination, control and exploitation, the same delusion that the Divine is elsewhere, the same blindfold.

Witches are growing wiser and the blindfolds are coming off. My sight returned with the simplest practices, many of which we all share—casting circle, honoring the four/six directions, grounding and centering, breathing, chanting, dancing, attuning body, psyche and soul to the great lunar rhythms and seasonal cycles. All within Esbat and Sabbat celebrations, journeying, meditating, working with altered states and spirits of place, and rather than projecting my will outward, I opened my heart and invited Divinity in.

I saw the unseen. I saw the Sacred, in realms of spirit and even a spark of it in myself. But most importantly, when I returned to this world and spent time in Nature, I saw the Sacred embodied by the natural world. Creation makes the unseen visible. Mother Earth gives life to energy, gives beauty to possibility, and wisdom to those who'll pay attention. Although we lost much over centuries of persecution and suppression, we have the same wise spiritual teacher as our indigenous ancestors, that all peoples have—Nature.

Nature taught me that I too was Nature. Awakening, I asked myself: how do I live knowing that my breath is Air, my blood is Water, my body is Earth and my energy, my spirit is Fire? What is the right way for me to live as part of Nature? Knowing that Nature embodies divinity, how do I live within a sacred world? How do I make magic?

Nature answers with laws that are simultaneously practical and profound spiritual principles. A template for the energies of life, I am an advocate for the alchemy of one in particular, what some biologists call "Nature's secret magic": That all living things, when taking care of themselves, make the world in which they live better for all Life.

That is divine magic.

When the blindfold comes off, we realize that magic is not something we do to control or manipulate unseen forces, seen forms or the Sacred. Witches don't use the elements. We don't exploit Air, Fire, Water and Earth, or their spirits, to do our bidding. We work with them, in partnership, experiencing their life-blessing powers as they carry us beyond the limits of our singular forms into the vast Life of Creation. With humility, reverence and respect we ask for assistance and we give back with gratitude, doing our part to sustain Nature's life-sustaining balance.

Magic is what happens when we experience the divinity of life. Magic is the energy that flows into and through our lives when the Sacred becomes embodied. Magic is a divine quality of life; it is love. And when we make magic with the Sacred, we discover that the first thing magic changes is us.

Mother Earth is showing us how to live within and as part of a sacred world. We are Nature embodying the Sacred, the vessel where energy and earth are one, the altar where the unseen becomes visible through us. We are divine magic flowing into life, into Creation.

Nature teaches us to live and make magic guided by the embodied divinity of Life. Nature's law offers us a simple but profound ethical principle: I seek to live in a sacred way, taking care of myself in ways that make the world a better place for all Life, because I am part of a sacred world.

Witches need Nature's secret magic and the world needs her Witches. Scientists are confirming what our indigenous sisters and brothers have been warning of: the future of life on Mother Earth is imperiled and we have only a short time to fix what we have broken and to live in a sacred way. Everything we need is all around and within us. Remove your blindfold, learn from Nature and the magic will begin.

—PHYLLIS CUROTT

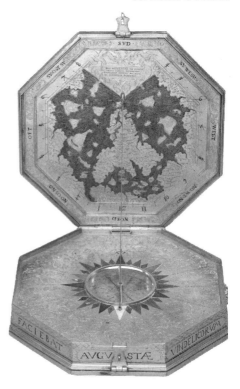

The Food of the Gods

Making offerings to the Orìṣá of Yorubaland

THE YORÙBÁ of Southwestern Nigeria have long had a unique relationship with their deities known as Irúnmọlè or Oriṣá. Unlike their high God Òlódùmaré who has no preferences and is not propitiated directly, the Oriṣá have preferences and offerings are made to them regularly. While not all are initiated into the mysteries of the individual Oriṣá, many maintain home shrines or propitiate them using items that are symbolic of a particular Oriṣá.

A common offering to Oriṣá is cool water, the sustenance of all life. Equally important are celebratory meals that are shared with the Oriṣá. While a blood sacrifice is typically only done by an Oloriṣá (initiated priest of Oriṣá) or by a Bàbáláwo/ Ìyánífá (priest or priestess of Ọrúnmìlà), simple offerings and the sharing of foods are commonly done by the lay population. Below are some of the items that are sacred to the individual Oriṣá and the particular foods that they enjoy, as well as the items that are taboo to offer to the very same Oriṣá.

Orí

Orí is the highest and most important of all the deities. It is the extension of Òlódùmaré in us. It is also the custodian of human destiny. Each human is born with this Oriṣá that is peculiar to them.

Orí is represented with cowries and skin in the form of a crown. The person whose Orí is being fed will sit while the priest will stand for the entire ceremony. The individual does not prostrate.

Orí lives on the head of each individual. Orí does not have a place in nature where offerings are placed. All would be presented to the head of the aboriṣá and then taken into the wild and left for natural forces to take it back.

Food items include kolanuts, bitter kola, alligator pepper, water, palm oil, liquor, white pigeon, guinea fowl,

duck, coconut, ram, honey and salt. It is taboo to offer palm kernel oil to Orí.

Èṣú

There is nothing that can be accomplished without the participation of Èṣú. He is the gate keeper for all that was, is and shall be. Èṣú embodies the principal of potential in the universe. His presence is so pervasive it is said that no one can truly list all of his names and attributes. In the beginning of time it was through the agency of the pervasive will and energy known as Àṣẹ that Òlódùmaré created all that is with the assistance of Èṣú. Until the end of time it is Èṣú, the gatekeeper and guardian of Àṣẹ, who will facilitate creation for Òlódùmaré. In all ceremonies Èsú is praised and extolled at the beginning and at the end.

As gatekeeper, Èṣú is the intermediary between Òlódùmaré and all the Orìṣá and between all the Orìṣá and mankind. While Ọrúnmìlà bears the messages of Òlódùmaré, it is Èṣú who carries the necessary sacrifices to the heavens when they are made. So integral are the messages of Òlódùmaré and the accompanying sacrifices that Èṣú and Ọrúnmìlà are always together and are the best of friends.

Symbols of Èṣú are the hooked dancing wand, yangi (laterite stone), a special curved knife known as Òbẹ Èṣú, and cloth that is black and red. Offerings are made to Èṣú while standing, his objects are never kept in the house, rather they are outside. Offerings are first presented to the back of the neck of the individual making the offering and then given to Èṣú. His offerings can be made at crossroads in the absence of his symbols.

Food items offered to Èṣú are kolanuts, bitterkola, pigeon, rooster, he-goat, guinea fowl, beans, fish, rat, pounded yam, Àmàlà (yam flower porridge) and Èkọ (fermented maize pudding). Taboos are the same as those for Ọrúnmìlà.

Ọrúnmìlà

Ọrúnmìlà is the deity of Wisdom. He is the wisest of the Orìṣá and is the messenger of Òlódùmaré, bringing the coded message of the heavens to the Earth. He guards and guides humans through his coded messages deciphered by his priests.

Ọrúnmìlà and Ifá are represented by Ikin, the sacred palm nuts from the palm tree know as Ope Ifá. His sacred vessel is maintained by his priests and his offerings are made to the Ikin. An offering made to him by an aborisà may be placed on a the ground calling to Ọrúnmìlà to accept the offering. Offerings to him are always made kneeling.

Food items offered to Ọrúnmìlà are kolanuts, bitter kola, palm oil, liquor, hen, she goat, bush rat, fish, pigeon, Àmàlà (yam flour porridge), Iyan (pounded yam) and Oka (cassava porridge). Taboo is Palm kernel oil,

Obàtálá

This Orisà is one of the most important of all the deities. Because of his favored status with the *source of all*, Òlódùmaré, he is given special reverence by all. It was Obàtálá who formed the Earth and the first to set foot on it. Obàtálá was responsible for molding humans from the clay of the river, breathing life into his creations. His unfortunate episode of drunkenness while doing such work is the cause of deformity in mankind. On seeing what resulted from his inebriation, he swore to never drink again and took all those who are deformed to be his special children.

Obàtálá is honest at all times and reverent at all times. His followers are expected to emulate his piety and purity. They are required to wear white often and are forbidden to drink or do mind-altering substances to the point of inebriation.

Symbols of Obàtálá are a calabash painted white filled with Ẹfun (naturally occurring white chalk), a leaden image of a human. In the absence of these, Obàtálá offerings can be made on the ground. Offerings to Obàtálá are made while kneeling in front of his objects.

Food offerings for Obàtálá are snails, chalk, shea butter, white goat, white hen, white kola nuts, pounded yam.

Taboos are palm wine or any alchoholic beverage, palm oil, palm kernel oil, salt, pork, stale water.

Ṣàngó

Ṣàngó is the Orisà in charge of rainfall and thunder/lightning. He is a deity that enforces morality and is petitioned for victory over adversaries, matters of fertility and issues of productivity. One of his appellations, Ewélérè (herbs are profitable) indicates that he can also be called upon to impart knowledge of herbs. Ṣàngó is the first of Kings to inhabit the

Earth. He is invoked and praised at all coronations of kings.

Symbols of Ṣangó are Oṣé Ṣangó (a double ax), Ẹdun Ara (thunder stones) mortar and pestle, a calabash filled of camwood dust. Offerings to Ṣangó are always made standing.

Food items offered to Ṣangó are bitterkola, rooster, ram, palm oil, àmàlà (yam flower porridge), gbẹ̀gìrì (bean soup), he-goat, roasted beans. His taboos are palm kernel oil, kolanuts, ewe, she-goat and hen.

Ògún

Ògún is the Oriṣá of metal, technology and industriousness. Ògún while being a warrior, is also the inventor of the metal technology used to produce farming implements. It is Ògún who leads all through the dense forest of decision, showing all the way forward.

Ògún is the Oriṣá who provided the 16 metal rods that were used to mold the skeletons of man and woman.

Among the objects that represent Ògún are knives and all objects made of iron. Often the "shrine" of Ògún will have a broad flat piece of iron.

Offerings are made to Ògún standing, usually taking place in the early morning. The offering items are placed on an iron object or placed at the foot of the akòko tree (*Newbouldia laevis*), a good substitute in northern environments is the tabebuia (also known as "roble"). A hole in the ground is also an appropriate place of offering.

Food items offered to Ògún are: raffia, palm wine, snail, tortoise, pounded yam, kola nut and bitterkola, palm oil, roasted yam, he goat, ram, rooster and pigeon. His taboos are all female animals, palm kernel oil and whistling in his presence.

Oṣún

In the beginning of time, 401 Oriṣá were sent to the Earth. Among them the only female divinity was Oṣún. Because the male Oriṣá decided Oṣún need not participate in decision making, Oṣún withdrew her support and departed. From that moment, not a single endeavor succeeded. The Oriṣá petitioned Òlódùmaré for help. Òlódùmaré asked where was the female that was sent with them. Apprised of the situation, Òlódùmaré told them they would always fail without female help.

Oṣún was the first of the Oriṣá to study Ifá with Orúnmìlà. He gave her the 16 cowries to use when consulting Ifá. She in turn taught the other Oriṣá to use the cowries.

Among the objects that represent Oṣún is a pot containing water (this is her medicine), eight brass fans, ivory hair combs and large white plates that hold her other sacred object. Offerings to Ọṣún are made mostly to her sacred pot which is placed into a hole dug in into the ground.

Offerings made to Ọṣún can be made to a river or to the ground. Offerings can also be made to a large white plate on which several of her objects can be placed. She is fed while keeling before her symbols or before a river.

Food items offered to Ọṣún are kolanuts, bitter kolanuts, hens, goat, èkọ (fermented maize pudding), pounded yam, yánrin (dandelion greens are a good North American substitute), sweet liquors and gin, palm oil. Her taboos are millet beer, duck and palm kernel oil.

Yemọja

While Yemọja is not considered to be Irúnmọlẹ̀ by many (Orìṣá that issued directly from Òlódùmaré), there is indications otherwise. In the story of the creation of mankind, she was Obàtálá's wife. Yemọja accompanied him to the Earth and assisted him in molding the humans from river clay. Being a riverine deity, she used her sacred waters to smooth the figures before Òlódùmaré breathed life into each. She is acclaimed to be the mother of all by many in Yorubaland. She is known throughout the land as the Orìṣá who has boundless patience and compassion.

Yemọja has incredibly strong connections with her sister Ọṣún. Both of whom are prayed to for fertility. Depending on what myth you read, Yemọja is said to be either the mother or the stepmother of Ṣangó. In either case, she has a special place in her heart for those who are initiated into Ṣangó's mysteries.

Among the objects that represent Yemọja are a camwood stained set of Ikin that have been strung into a necklace. Depending on where you are, a vessel filled with water from the Ògún river or from the ocean is a symbol of her mysteries. A blue stained handwoven cloth is also one of her symbols. Her offerings are made by a river with one of her symbols or beside a pèrègún tree, an evergreen that is common in Yorubaland. Making offerings to her are made kneeling down and some of the offerings may be placed directly in a river (if available.)

Food items offered to Yemọja are white kolanuts, liquor, palm oil, sugar cane, snail, yánrin, èkuru (ground cooked beans) and palm oil. Her taboos are fish, bitter kola, tobacco, guinea corn and palm kernel oil.

—IFADOYIN SANGOMUYIWA

Bó bá digbá bo Ifá è

A gúnyán sílè rábàtà

Gbogbo èèyán ó bàá móo wá jeun

Ení ó bà sì yawó

Tí n se nnkan rere

Nnkan rere nínlá náà níí rí

Bí gbogbowón bá jeun tán

When it is time for him to observer his festival of Ifá

He would prepare a lot of pounded yam

Everyone would come to his house to eat

And he that is generous

And also doing good things

Would get good things also in bundles

When all of them had food to eat

They would start to pray for him

Excerpt from Òsá Ìretè an Ese Ifá
(divination poem)

The Mysteries & Myths of Moldavite

MOLDAVITE IS OFTEN referred to as a stone, but it's actually a glass that was created about 14.8 million years ago when a large meteorite crashed into the Czech Republic. The impact from the collision was so strong that both the meteorite and the land it crashed into vaporized upon impact. This vaporized rock eventually liquefied and rained down from the sky, cooling and solidifying into an aerodynamic shape before it hit the Earth again as the rare green glass known as moldavite.

Because of its rarity and popularity among Witches, mystics and healers, moldavite can be fairly expensive. Moldavite's popularity is not because it's rare though, but rather because of the high vibrational quality which the stone emits. Among its properties, moldavite enhances psychism, healing abilities, induces astral projection and out-of-body experiences, accelerates one's life lessons and opens one up to deeper levels of awareness and compassion.

However, it isn't just new agers and Neopagans that have revered Moldavite for its spiritual abilities and associations. We see evidence of the glass being incorporated into the religious aspects of the ancient Neolithic people of Eastern Europe 25,000 years ago. These people crafted and wore moldavite as spiritual talismans and amulets for good fortune and fertility. In 1908 Johann Veran discovered a statue during excavations conducted by archaeologists Josef Szombathy, Hugo Obermaier and Josef Bayer at a paleolithic site near Willendorf, a village in Lower Austria. The statue was named the Venus of Willendorf and is believed to be the oldest image of a deity on Earth.

The name Venus was used around this time period to indicate that it was an "immodest" Goddess—having no connection to the Roman Goddess of the same name. The figure was believed to be a fertility deity, speculated to be the Paleolithic *Magna Mater* or Great

Mother Goddess of ancient people. What is less known about the discovery of this Goddess is that in the same excavation they found many talismans, amulets and ritual knives crafted from Moldavite. The two seemed to share a significant link, indicating that it was most likely sacred to the fertility Goddess.

The *Tabula Smaragdina* or *Emerald Tablet*, a condensed piece of the Hermetica, contains the foundational secret knowledge of alchemy and the Hermetic Tradition. The text is believed to explain in cryptic language the secrets of *prima materia* and its transmutation to create the fabled Philosopher's Stone, as well as an understanding of macrocosmic and microcosmic forces. This knowledge was inscribed on an "emerald that fell from heaven." Some believe the tablet wasn't carved on emerald at all, but rather moldavite.

It is interesting to note that many ancient people referred to any transparent green stone as "emerald." The text of the *Emerald Tablet* seems to reflect the creation of moldavite itself. Perhaps the text explaining the creation of the spiritual Lapis Elixir (The Philosopher's Stone) was carved on the physical Philosopher's Stone itself. Legends tells us that when Lucifer fell from heaven, Archangel Michael swung his sword at Lucifer's crown and an emerald fell out, hitting the Earth. This legendary emerald was symbolic of the fall of humanity and also the key to humanity's redemption. In legend this emerald was the Holy Grail itself.

Moldavite also has been theorized to be Cintamani of Buddhist lore. In the 1920s a high abbot from the Trasilumpo lamasery was said to have entrusted Nicholas Roerich, a Russian artist and explorer, with a fragment of the Cintamani. Roerich speculated that the stone was moldavite which had a sanskrit inscription he translated as *"Through the Stars I come. I bring the chalice covered with the shield. Within it I bring a treasure, the gift of Orion."*

That earliest temple to Artemis/Diana of Ephesus supposedly contained a sacred stone that had "fallen from Jupiter" called the *diopet* and was later reportedly placed within the tower-like crown of the statue of Artemis/Diana. It was held as being a divine object, not only because it fell from the sky, but because it resembled Artemis/Diana of Ephesus. The diopet held such reverence that it was paired together with the statue of Artemis/Diana in Acts 19:35 in the Bible, *"And when the town clerk had appeased the people, he said, ye men of Ephesus, what man is there that knoweth not how that the city of the Ephesians is a worshipper of the great goddess Diana, and of her image which fell down from Jupiter?"*

The City of Liverpool Museum acquired a stone from antiquarian Charles Seltman who bought it at Ephesus in the 1940s, claiming that it was the diopet. Elizabeth Pepper and John Wilcock wrote in *Magical and Mystical Sites: Europe and the British Isles* that the stone was some sort of neolithic volcanic greenstone and that iron bands were added, which were the same as found in meteorites. It isn't that far of a stretch to speculate that the diopet might be moldavite.

−MAT AURYN

witches, Bitches, twitches

William Gray and Witches

WILLIAM G. GRAY, or Bill to his friends, was a brilliant, talented, and sometimes opinionated ceremonial magician who fought the Nazis in WWII. In the ensuing years after the war, he wrote books, performed rituals and interacted with some of the biggest names in modern occult history. The following is a snippet from his biography *The Old Sod: The Odd Life and Inner Work of William G. Gray.*

I'm afraid I've seen and heard so much bloody rubbish masquerading as Sex Magic, that I'm just about disenchanted with the topic. I think of the great Aleister Crowley sitting up in bed casting I Ching sticks to decide whether or not he wakes Leah up to poke her or not. I think of skinny old Gerald Gardner King(?) of the Witches prancing around with elk-horns from a coat-rack tied on his head while the girls tickle his tool with a pink feather-duster. I think of all these so-called Master Magicians and High Priests of Witch Covens living on National Assistance and trying to convince themselves they are Adepts and God knows what of Sex magic when they couldn't even raise a good fart between the lot — let alone anything more dangerously fertile. All because of a pathetic peurility and a lack of genuine love anywhere. Poor, poor little people. God grant them love in their next life-rounds. They need it desperately.

[letter to AR 1/11/72]

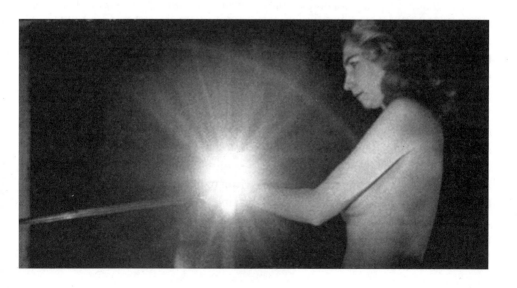

"I've metaphorically booted more would-be occultists out of my doors than I can remember. Witches, bitches, twitches, and all their odd little itches I couldn't care less about. (Though I've met most of the self-styled 'witches,' and actually kept on more or less friendly terms with rare examples.)" So he wrote in an undated letter to Alan Richardson in 1969.

Of all the different kinds of occultist that he met, he really did seem to be able to relate to the witches better than anyone. Although he had a reputation in his later life for falling out with absolutely everyone, he never had a bad word to say about Doreen Valiente, E.A. St George, or Pat and Arnold Crowther—all of whom were heavily involved in what has been seen as the rebirth of the Craft. He also knew and worked with Robert Cochrane and became slightly bewildered by the cult status that the younger man rapidly started to achieve after his untimely death. All of them worked differing kinds of magic together. Things passed between them on magical levels. If, in a formal way, the druids had once made him their 'Distinguished Stranger,' then the completely informal witches used him—unconsciously—in exactly the same way as he attended the rebirth of their own religion.

Perhaps he got on so well with them because these pioneers of post-War witchcraft were as busy evolving their systems as he was, and he saw them as kindred spirits. Or perhaps because the witches related to him on less cerebral and more affectionate levels, and were not seen as threats.

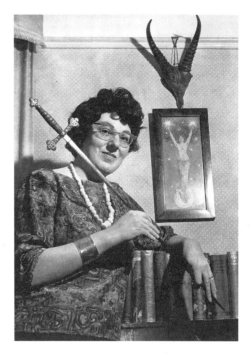

However Bill detested the actual word 'witch', despite getting on very well with the witches themselves. You had only to drop the 'W' word into the conversation and he would rise to the bait every time, launching into a fiery and exasperated monologue about the sheer wrongness of the term. There was something of the amateur etymologist about the man; in fact he once argued that an etymological dictionary should be a compulsory item for anyone assaying the magical path.

One of the witches with whom he argued word meanings was the legendary Doreen Valiente, who might be regarded as the Founding Mother of the modern Craft, as they came to call it. She had been initiated by Gerald Gardner in 1953, and used her own very real talent for poetry to write and shape the so-called 'Book of Shadows.' She left Gardner's coven in 1957 and formed a daughter coven of her own. In 1964 she was initiated by Robert Cochrane into what the latter termed a traditional, hereditary branch of witchcraft. After her death in 1999 she left behind a series of excellent books on the topic, and a large number of devoted followers.

"We grew fond of Doreen from the start although we had endless arguments on the topic of the word 'Witch.' She would persist in calling herself such despite all we could do to persuade her otherwise. In the end it was she herself who mentioned that the American folklorist Leland had first claimed this meant a 'Wise person,' and everyone since had simply taken his word for it. In fact Leland had made a sad little mistake in confusing the Anglo-Saxon term 'wicce' (wicked one) with 'witega' (wise one) and assumed that the modern spelling of our word 'witch' must mean a wise person, whereas it means a wicked person in the sense of being a weak one. Any good Anglo-Saxon dictionary should· clear this point in moments. Increasing numbers are beginning to realise this and drop the 'witch' description of themselves in favour of the word 'Pagan,' which is perfectly permissible though etymologically incorrect."

Fortunately Bill died before he saw the upsurge in those Witch movements which he in no small part influenced—directly or otherwise, wittingly or no—or had to endure the myriad books with that dreaded word writ large upon the covers.

Ronald Hutton, the Professor of History at the University of Bristol, did the first full-scale and scholarly study of what has been described as the only religion England has ever given to the world: modern pagan witchcraft. The resulting book *The Triumph of the Moon* might be regarded as the first real history of this new-born revelation, and although coolly objective throughout, it still manages to be sympathetic. On reading the book, despite all the squabbles and disagreements between the personalities, the outrageous claims and outright lies, it is hard not to come away impressed by the witch movement he so lucidly

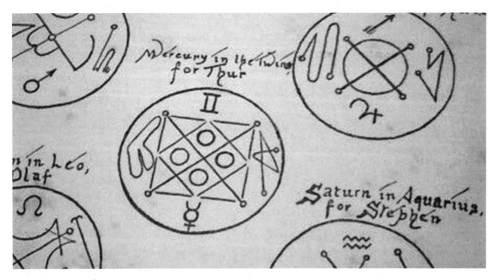

describes, with its underlying ethic of 'An it harm none, do what thou wilt...' Gray's assessment of the new religion was typical:

"What the whole cult really amounts to is a socio-religious protest against the so-called 'Establishment' of Church and State which seeks to impose a set of conventions on human society in expectation of conformity. There have always been sections of that society which resent and disagree with such impositions because they object to interference with their purely personal opinions. So they usually organise something which symbolically opposes the overall rule of the prevailing majority. Almost anything to distinguish themselves from the mass of mankind forming the bulk of human beings. What they become depends on the degree and inclination they decide to follow. Those calling themselves Witches nowadays would have called themselves something quite different in former times. In my mothers day they would have been 'Bohemians,' in earlier times Adamites, and all down the ages they have called themselves whatever seemed appropriate for their era. The Church called them heretics, the Law knew them as malefactors, Politics described them as revolutionaries or reformers. However they termed themselves, they were just humans who determined to be different and the way in which they tried this provided a name for their methodology."

He went on to give some more unique insights into this delightful woman with whom he often crossed swords:

"Doreen was a very genuine scholar with one of the best private libraries on occult topics which I have encountered. She was a very tall woman of just over six feet, who married a very small Spaniard who worked as a chef, and had been a rebel in the Spanish Civil War. This was Cassie, short for Casimir. Although he understood English perfectly, his pronounced accent was so strong and fast that I could never understand him. He took no part in Doreen's 'witchcraft,' but made no attempt to interfere with it, being of atheistical persuasion. She sometimes called him her dear little gnome, lifted him by both elbows to kiss him and then sat him in his favourite chair to watch TV while we would follow her into their bedroom, to talk without its interference. His great passion was watching all-in wrestling, and his pet budgerigar would fly out of its cage to join him on his shoulder, and the sight of the small man and his tiny bird bouncing up and down with excitement together while horrendous howls came from the box was highly amusing."

And then there was Pat Crowther (née Dawson), who had the traditionally fey Breton forebears. She too had been initiated by Gardner, in 1960, and was seen by many as his spiritual heir. And in turn Pat initiated her husband, Arnold. During the rite she had a powerful trance experience in which she saw herself as being reborn into the Moon Mysteries, passed gauntlet-style through the spread legs of a line of howling, naked women. Apart from the teachings she received from Gardner, an old witch from Inverness (whom she called simply Jean), passed on what she said was a 300 year old secret inner tradition. Her husband Arnold (1909–1974), so often overshadowed by his famous wife, was a remarkable man in his own right. In a previous age he might have been termed a Cunning Man, and in this one showed a passion for stage magic, ventriloquism, sleight-of-hand, puppeteering and illusions generally. He also had very clear memories of his past lives and was keenly aware that beneath the legerdemain, there was another kind of magic, and other worlds. He introduced Gerald Gardner to Aleister Crowley in 1946, thus creating the speculations about the latter's involvement with the former which have endured to this day. Delightfully, he died on the ancient feast of Beltane (May 1st), and was given rites appropriate to a member of the Old Religion.

"Pat Crowther had a magnificent singing voice, and had at one time been one of 'Mr Cochranes Young Ladies' but had quitted that company to marry Arnold, a much older man who practiced ventriloquism and conjuring at which he was highly talented. Pat still took Principle Boy's parts in pantomime, and they sometimes together worked to run holiday camps in British summer resorts. They were seldom without an engagement somewhere, and from time to time would visit us in Cheltenham celebrating Seasonal Rites there."

Both Pat and Bill did a lot of work in respect to the sonic aspects of magic — the so-called 'Words of Power' — and in particular the use of the vowels to link with elemental forces. It is hard to read Pat's analyses without imagining Bill; when you study Bill's work you cannot fail to visualise Pat.

—MARCUS CLARIDGE AND
ALAN RICHARDSON

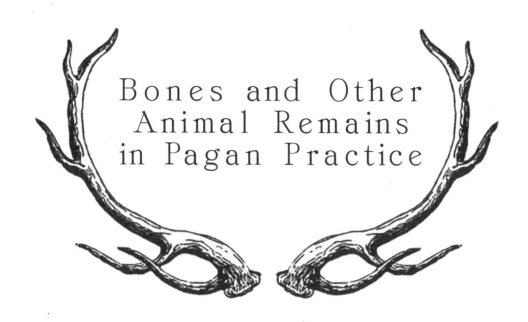

Bones and Other Animal Remains in Pagan Practice

DEATH IS A NATURAL part of the life cycle which each and every one of us must someday face. Those who revere nature do not shy away from this reality, but instead embrace it as having equal value to birth and life. Some choose to take on the task of caring for the remains of the deceased, at least those of a non-human persuasion.

These sacred remains—bones, hides, feathers and more—are an important part of the legacy of Witchcraft and nature-based religions. They composed some of the earliest religious items humanity crafted, to say nothing of mundane tools and needs. And they served as a daily reminder of our interdependence with the rest of nature, something modern plastic cannot do. Of course, the 21st century also brings with it the discussion of whether animal remains can still be ethically procured, and who gets to decide what is "ethical."

For those who do include the respectful integration of hide and bone with altar and ritual, the first question is where to procure the remains. A walk in the woods may reveal bones, antlers and feathers, though the internet also provides a myriad of curiosities dealers who will provide all manner of specimens at a price. Other sources include antique shops (excellent for finding vintage taxidermy) and thrift stores (old fur coats can be altered and incorporated into ritual wear). Omnivores may even wish to honor the bones of animals who fed them.

This honor can be given in any number of ways. Animal remains can be easily incorporated into an altar, shrine or other sacred space. They also work well as ritual tools in and of themselves. A long bone or antler may become a suitable wand or the handle for an athame. Bull and bison horns can be polished and waxed to become ritual vessels, and some leather hides are more than suitable for binding a grimoire or other sacred book.

When performing rituals, particularly those within a sacred space, the spirits of the hides and bones should be included in any acknowledgement of esoteric beings. Additionally, ask the spirits whose remains compose ritual tools to join in the work at hand. A little acknowledgement can go a long way.

One practice to keep in mind is that of purification. While all animal remains are inherently sacred, they may carry the energies of bad deaths. Upon acquiring a new hide, bone or other part, take time to meditate with it. Ask it if it would like to show you anything about its life or death, or to tell you anything else important. Some are reluctant to speak, at least at first. Others may be quite willing to have someone listen to them.

Once this conversation has happened, purify the remains by passing them through the smoke of herbs such as sage or cedar. Say a prayer that they may be at home with you, or that through you they may find the best place to be with someone who loves and appreciates them. Ask if there is a particular offering the spirits may appreciate in particular.

Generally speaking, the remains have little use for direct offerings such as libations or food; however, they often welcome offerings made on the part of their living relatives. Feeding wildlife (especially wild mammals) generally encourages them to lose their fear of humans and become dependent on us. Instead, consider making a donation to or volunteering time with a conservation organization that protects wildlife and their habitats.

In the event that a particular hide or bone wishes to be put to rest, perform a ritual of gratitude and honor. Then leave it in as wild a place as possible to decay back into the ground. Make sure that as many human-made elements have been removed as possible. Painted skulls and bones, for example, should have their paint stripped, and any plastic buttons or metal zippers on hide garments should be taken off. Don't bury the remains, as living wildlife can make use of these resources. Bones are full of calcium that many animals need, and hides and feathers provide bedding. The best care

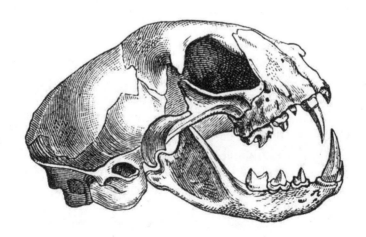

should be offered to these remains during their entire tenure of spiritual service.

What does that service look like more specifically? What can be done with various bits of hide and bone and such? Here are some ideas:

Hides: This refers to the tanned or otherwise preserved hide of an animal. Hair-on hide is known as fur, while hide with the hair removed is leather, or rawhide if it has not been fully tanned. Rawhide, of course, makes excellent drumskins, but can also be formed into folded pouches. Tanned hides also make excellent material for sewing bags to hold sacred items of all sorts. A large hide drapes over an altar nicely as a cloth, though be careful when using candles so as to not burn it or get wax in the hair. Some people also may wear hides as headdresses and other garments. Try incorporating smaller bits of hide and hair into a spell pouch to add the animal's energy to your intent, or wrapping a candle in hide overnight to absorb its energy before burning it (without the hide, of course). A taxidermy mount is a dramatic and impressive way to bring a hide into a ritual setting, whether on its own or adorned in other sacred items.

Bones, Horns, Teeth and Claws: Harder items are a common component of ritual jewelry. Smaller bones, teeth and claws are ready to drill and string onto a cord, though larger bones, antlers and horns may need to be cut down to size. Bones, antlers and horns also make excellent handles for athames and other ritual tools. A few hooves tied to leather straps and dangled from a handle create a beautifully organic rattle. Hang an antler or horn at your front door for protection, or on the bedroom door for fertility. A

string of claws or teeth can be worn as a necklace for further protective energy, or to carry the strength of the animals with you into challenging situations. Bones in particular are a connection to evolutionary ancestor spirits from well before humans came to be. Skulls seem to have the most compelling power of all, as they are the center of the senses. They make excellent guardians at the quarters and elsewhere in the ritual space, and may also be used in divination.

Feathers: Rightfully, often associated with the element of Air, feathers are also among the easiest animal remains to collect and preserve (keeping legalities in mind). They are naturally molted seasonally, and are simple to clean. They can be stored in a vase or other container just about anywhere, and don't require anything except occasional dusting. Whole wings need to be dried in a box of salt or Borax for several weeks so that the flesh is desiccated. Feathers make excellent fans for directing the smoke from burnt herbs and incense, or otherwise sending energy on its way. They are also quite ornamental and make excellent ritual decorations and personal adornments. As they are lightweight they can even be braided into long hair, or in witches' ladders and other magical cords.

Shells: Many spiritual practitioners use abalone shells to hold sage and other incense while it burns, but that's just the beginning. Larger shells (both seashells and turtle shells) make good containers for crystals, herbs and other small items. Watertight ones can serve as vessels for ritual libations, though these should not be consumed for germy reasons. A turtle shell full of soil makes a perfect representation of the element of Earth, while an abalone with water embodies that western Element. When collecting shells on the shoreline, make sure there is nothing living inside of them. Be aware that many commercially available seashells were not sustainably collected; the animals in them may have been killed, and populations of some species (such as the nautilus) are endangered due to too much demand for their shells. Better to collect them yourself or seek them secondhand in antique shops and thrift stores.

Preserved insects and other arthropods: Most animal remains used in ritual are from vertebrates; however, invertebrates leave behind intricate exoskeletons. Sometimes this is something as simple as a dead fly or bee on a window sill, or a butterfly wing left over from a bird's meal out in the garden. Some purveyors of curiosities also sell museum-quality specimens, though again be very cautious about sourcing.

Most supposedly "farmed" butterflies are actually caught in the wild and killed to meet the demand for specimens and wings for jewelry. Preserved arthropods are very delicate, so they should be kept on an altar or other surface where they won't be crushed or disturbed, and only handled minimally.

Flesh: Many people don't often think of meat as animal parts, but that's because we have a tendency to be separated from the sources of our food—animal and plant alike. Yet omnivores are consuming something that is as much a part of an animal as hide or bone. Other foodstuffs come from animals, like eggs, dairy products, honey, and gelatin (made from hooves). The spiritual side of cooking is something that has been expounded upon in many books and articles, but what is often omitted is how to honor the animals whose remains are being cooked. There is no single correct answer to this, it's all about intent. Prepare the meat and other food with care and reverence, and focus on taking the energy of this animal into your own body to become a part of you. Carefully dispose of anything left over such as bones, preferably through burial or compost. When possible, select meat and other animal products from small, local farms that raise their animals in pastures instead of feedlots, or even raise your own if that's an option.

These are just a few of the ways in which animal remains may be respectfully incorporated into spiritual practice. The important thing to remember is to honor the wishes of the spirits within these remains, and to treat them with the utmost respect.

—LUPA

Merry Meetings

*A candle in the window, a fire on the hearth,
a discourse over tea…*

SELENA FOX has been on the forefront of the Pagan Movement in the Untied States since the early 70s. Leading her first public pagan ritual in 1971, she can be counted among the prominent elders in the Pagan and Ecospirituality communities. Because of Selena's efforts as a public media spokesperson and religious freedom activists, Pagans in the United States have begun to realize freedoms that other religious communities enjoy. It was *CIRCLE Magazine* and *Circle Guide to Pagan Groups* that guided many seekers of Paganism and Wicca to a spiritual home. Selena is also a trained counselor and psychotherapist receiving a B.S. cum laude in psychology from the College of William & Mary and an M.S. in counseling from the University of Wisconsin-Madison where her thesis was entitled When Goddess is God: Pagans, Recovery, and Alcoholics Anonymous.

At the time of your birth, your family members were observant conservative Southern Baptists. Can you tell us about the journey that took you elsewhere?

I began having lucid dreams, out of body travel, and encounters with Nature spirits as a young child. At the age of nine, I had a mystical experience that included a calling to ministry, and as a result, I deepened my involvement with my family's church and Christian studies. However, as I matured, I came to realize that since I was female, I would not be able to be an ordained Southern Baptist minister. When I was seventeen, I left the church, expanded my spiritual studies, and changed my religious identification from Baptist to Pantheist, a philosophy with origins in ancient Paganism.

Your membership in the Eta Sigma Phi Honor Society indicates that you studied Classics. Did your studies lead to research of classical religious beliefs and how did this inform your developing practices?

I took my first course in Latin and Classics when I was thirteen. I enjoyed it so much that I continued my studies through high school and college, deepening my affinity with ancient Roman and Greek cultures, philosophy, and religion. During my undergraduate years at the College of William and Mary, I was active in organizing Classics activities, including founding the Classics Club, and serving as President of the campus chapter of Eta Sigma Phi. During my senior year, I got the idea to complement Classics classroom work with experiential learning. With the support and participation of Classics Department faculty and students, I created and facilitated a Greco-Roman Rite of Spring. Dressed in tunics and togas, we processed to a green space in the center of campus and invoked Dionysus and Gaea/Terra in an ecstatic ceremony. What was a fun, educational experience that day for our group, also set me on my priestess path. I called the Ancient Ones, and They came—and They have been part of my life ever since.

Can you tell us a bit about the hereditary Witch that you met in Hampton, Virginia and her effect on your own journey?

My first job after college graduation in 1971 was working on an archaeological dig in Hampton Roads. I became friends with a co-worker, Marianne, and we discovered that we had

a shared interest in magick. She was a family tradition Witch with Prussian heritage. She invited me to her home, and on Full Moon nights we did ceremony together. Sometimes other women would join us. Through our relationship, I learned some magickal ways of working with the Moon as well as the joys of working with other Pagans in a small group.

You define yourself as a Wiccan priestess, rather than a Witch. What are the distinguishing differences separating the two definitions?

I identify both with Wiccan priestess and Witch, and for me personally, I view them as interchangeable terms. However, I know that for some, these terms are not interchangeable. In the 1970s and early 1980s, I used Witch

publicly to identify myself more often than Wiccan priestess. However, that changed as I became increasingly active in Pagan religious freedom and civil rights work. I found it more politically effective to be publicly identified as a Wiccan priestess in order to work for equal rights for Witches, Wiccans, and other Pagans.

Can you tell us about how Circle Sanctuary went from concept to reality?

I founded Circle Sanctuary at Samhain time in 1974. Its original name, Circle, and the logo of a circle containing twelve circles around a central circle came to me in a meditative vision along with the concept of creating a spiritual center that would bring together people who celebrated Nature in sacred ways. Six weeks later, I brought some friends together for Circle's first gathering, a Yuletide celebration. In June of 1975, Circle Sanctuary moved into its first rural home, a rented farmstead near Sun Prairie, Wisconsin. We created a ritual room on the main floor and a ritual circle outside. We began holding classes and seasonal celebrations there as well as in nearby Madison, Wisconsin. In 1978, we incorporated as a non-profit religious organization in Wisconsin and in 1980 received federal 501(c)(3) tax exempt church status. In 1983, we purchased and moved to our present home, Circle Sanctuary Nature Preserve, a 200-acre Nature sanctuary in southwestern Wisconsin.

How did the greater Pagan community help you realize this vision and how has the community benefited from Circle Sanctuary?

Over the years, we have had Pagans of many paths and places work with us on a variety of our projects and services, including publications, sacred sites preservation, festivals, civil rights activism, interfaith relations, academic studies, and podcasts. We continue to be thankful for contributions of time, money, expertise and other support we receive.

Circle Sanctuary has helped the greater Pagan community in a variety of ways. Through our Lady Liberty League, we have helped win Pagan civil rights and religious freedom victories. Through our events, websites, social media, podcasts, albums and publications, we have facilitated the sharing of rituals, music, art and knowledge in print, in person, and online by Pagans of many traditions across the USA and around the world. Every year, we sponsor training for Pagan leaders through the Pagan Leadership Institute we hold during our weeklong Pagan Spirit Gathering. We helped develop the emerging field of Pagan Studies in academia, including coordinating Pagan Academic Circle. We have established the first national Pagan cemetery and one of the first Pagan land projects. We have been among those sponsoring and supporting festivals and conferences bringing together Pagans from different paths. We continue to help bring about better public understanding and respect of Pagans and Paganism through interfaith networking and chaplaincy endorsement.

Lady Liberty League has done some very important work, can you tell about some

of the recent progress that Lady Liberty League benefits the broad spectrum of Paganism and Witchcraft.

Lady Liberty League (LLL), founded in 1985, is the Pagan civil rights and religious freedom support service of Circle Sanctuary. Over the years, we have helped Pagans across the United States and other countries combat discrimination, defamation and harassment. We helped win the ten-year battle to have the US Department of Veterans Affairs (VA) authorize the inclusion of the Pentacle on the memorial markers its issues to mark the graves of deceased veterans, and now more than 200 Pentacle-inscribed markers are in public and private cemeteries across the USA. In 2017, with the help of LLL and Circle Sanctuary, the Awen, a Druid symbol, was added to the VA's list of symbols authorized for memorial markers and several have been issued. In recent years, LLL's work also has included work with zoning, public

accommodation, child custody, inmate access to Pagan materials, and chaplaincy issues.

Can you tell us about your involvement in the first Earth Day in 1970?

I helped organize an environmental teach-in at the College of William and Mary on the first Earth Day, April 22, 1970, and I have been active in organizing Earth Day events ever since. We have a public Earth Day Festival every year at Circle Sanctuary Nature Preserve. In 2019, I taught a five-part EcoRites leadership intensive attended by Pagan leaders from across the USA and some other countries as part of preparations for the 50th Anniversary of Earth Day in 2020 and future Earth Days.

What are the current environmental endeavours that you and Circle Sanctuary are pursing?

We are engaged in a variety of environmental projects at Circle Sanctuary Nature Preserve, including forest preservation, wetlands conservation, prairie restoration, and Ecospiritual education. In addition, I do workshops and public talks on Greening the End of Life as well as direct Circle Cemetery, a national Pagan cemetery, which is one of the first Green cemeteries in North America.

Tell us about the Circle Craft Tradition and what distinguishes it from other Traditions?

Circle Craft is a form of spiritual practice which combines old and new Pagan folkways, shamanism, Wiccan spirituality, transpersonal psychology and Nature mysticism. I helped form this tradition in

1971 with its primary influences being from Greek and Roman Pagan religions, American folk magick of Appalachian and Ozark mountains, and American adaptions of folkways from Scotland, Germany and Latvia. Central to the Circle Craft tradition is Nature communion and the honoring of the Divine as One and as Many. The Wheel of the Year in the Circle Craft tradition begins with Samhain and includes Solstices, Equinoxes, and Cross Quarter Sabbats. Sabbat celebrations take place over several days and nights rather than on a particular day as is the case with some other traditions. Circle Craft practice also includes the celebration of the New and Full Moons. As with many Wiccan and Witchcraft traditions, ceremonies are held in a Circle which is cast clockwise. However, in Circle Craft practice, nine directions are called instead of just the four compass points of many traditions. The Nine directions and association sacred forces are: Earth, physical realm, in the North; Air, mental realm,

in the East; Fire, behavioural realm, in the South; Water, emotional realm, in the West; Cosmos, Universe, for Above; Planet, Biosphere, for Below; Spirit, Divine Unity, in the Center; Soul, Within; and Community, Around. Some traditions are initiatory, and some are non-initiatory. Both options exist in the Circle Craft tradition. The Circle Craft path has much in common with Hedgewitchery and contemporary multicultural Shamanism. It includes work with ancestors, green spirits, animal spirits, and spirits of place in addition to Elementals and Divinities.

Circle Guide to Wicca & Pagan Resources of the 70s and 80s which you compiled was an important tool for the new seeker on the Pagan path. What would you recommend for Pagans today taking their first steps, regarding both books and networking.

My recommendations for those new to Paganism include: (1) at the start of

each day, do a prayer, short meditation or ritual honoring the Divine by the name(s) that you connect most strongly with; (2) spend at least a few minutes every day in a park or garden, by a tree or body of water, or in some other natural setting communing with and appreciating being part of Nature; (3) select several Pagan articles and books in print and/or on line and read and study them; (4) also learn through Pagan podcasts and videos; (5) attend at least one festival or other event per year that brings together Pagans of different paths in order to experience Pagan diversity face-to-face; (6) also explore and experience Pagan diversity via social media and note which forms seem to be the most compatible for you; (7) keep a spiritual journal and note experiences, dreams, visions, perspectives, and ideas; (8) pay attention to dreams and daydreams and listen to their messages; and (9) create a personal altar to use as a focal point for practice.

There were many hotbeds of activity in the 70s and 80s, for instance the Magickal Childe, the burgeoning festival circuit and Circle Sanctuary. What do you see for the community that is in closer communication via the internet yet in many ways isolated?

Engaging with cyberspace makes it possible for Pagans to connect with much information and many people, but if Pagan contact is limited only to cyberspace, this can be isolating. Cyberspace can be a helpful tool but it is important to balance cyberspace with face-to-face encounters with other humans and the natural world.

Attending a Pagan festival, fair, concert, conference, pride day or other event can be a way to deepen awareness of the larger Pagan world and to make lasting, mutually beneficial, holistic connections.

Tell us about your continuing profession involving counseling, readings and life. How does this benefit you, your clients and the Pagan community?

Combining my professional training in psychology and spiritual studies, I do counseling, psychotherapy, readings and life coaching as part of my work. Most of my sessions with clients are done via telephone consultations; some are by zoom video conference. Most of my clients are in the United States, but I also have worked with clients from other countries. Clients seek me out for a variety of reasons. Some do work with me as part of a life passage, such as dealing with a birth, marriage, death, change in residence or job change. Some consult in order to work through a trauma or other challenge. Some do sessions with me in order to deepen their spiritual understanding. Some connect in order to get insights on dreams and visions they have had. I continue to learn and grow from this work and am thankful that I have been able to help others on their life journeys. As a mental health professional, I have done diversity education in hospitals, clinics and other health care facilities and I been able to help build bridges of understanding about Pagans and Paganism and to demonstrate how Pagan spirituality can be a positive aid to personal growth and development.

The Magic of Seashells & Fossils

MERE WEEKS after my mother gave birth to me, I was introduced to the ocean. The rough silky texture of sand between my toes and the sound and feel of the bubbling summer waves of the Atlantic became imprinted upon me. So it's probably not much of a surprise that I have long been fascinated by the many gifts of the water, especially seashells and other remnants of sea-life.

When you pick up a shell on the beach, have you ever thought about the life of the creature that once occupied it? Have you ever looked at a fossil and pondered the centuries that have passed by since the creature gave its last breath? While certainly any crystal or similar mineral has an energy to it, shells and fossils have a potency all their own, stemming from lived experience. Hence, they are well-suited for an array of magical uses.

You would be hard-pressed to find any culture on Earth that hasn't held a fascination with shells. While there is the obvious appreciation for marine life that is edible, it's the inedible, long-lasting parts that have drawn our attention in other ways. Seashells have been utilized in trade as a form of currency all over the globe, from the Americas to Africa and Asia. Their shape, accessibility, and durability enabled them to be among the earliest tools known to humanity. Not only used for practical means, prehistoric grave sites reveal that our ancestors fashioned shells into necklaces, bead-work on clothing, and adornment. These finds suggest that shells were not only cherished for their beauty, but also possibly associated with status or role, and used for protection, fertility and other charms. Such metaphysical connections are further underlined by the fact that seashells are still today made into ritual instruments, connected with deities, and incorporated into systems of divination across the world.

To understand how you can connect with the magic of seashells, let's take a closer look. "Seashell" typically refers to the exoskeleton of an invertebrate animal—essentially the hard, living, and protective outer layer of its body—and composed of calcium carbonate or chitin. When the animal has died and decomposed, the hard shell is what remains, very much like our own bones.

There are hundreds of thousands of species of mollusks and other shell-bearing creatures—freshwater, saltwater, and even on land. The ones you are probably most familiar with are the bivalves ("two parts") which is the heading that clams, mussels, scallops and oysters fall under, and the univalves ("one part") or gastropods ("stomach foot") which includes snails, conchs, limpets, abalone and cowries. There are also the tusk and tooth-shelled scaphopods ("boat foot"), the multi-plated chitons (polyplacophorans), and cephalopods ("head foot") which includes the nautilus and also squid, octopus and cuttlefish—which have internal shells. Outside of these groups, you're also likely to find the shell remains of crabs, sea urchins, barnacles, corals and sand dollars. Additionally, the most commonly found fossils are the ancestors of many of the aforementioned creatures.

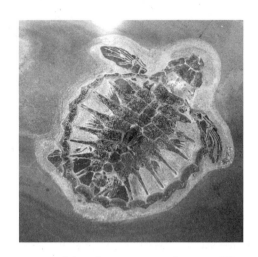

Spellcraft

As shells originally functioned to protect, they can easily be incorporated into spells of protection, worn as amulets, or fashioned into talismans. Often you can find half of a clam shell that already has a small hole near the top, making it easy to string up. The smooth interior is the perfect surface to draw or paint symbols and sigils on, and then seal them with clear nail polish. Still-connected bivalves could be used in love spells, balancing dualities, or workings where you need two parts brought together.

Snails can represent "bringing home with you"—so their shells make excellent travel charms, as well as a way to draw a safe place to you. Also, they can symbolize taking a slow and steady path, perfect for when you need to calm the pace of something. These shells can be painted or packed with herbs as needed. The shape of many snail shells and nautili also form the Fibonacci spiral (the golden ratio), another way to tap into universal energy for spellcraft.

There's also the cowrie shell with its unique rounded, vulva-like shape which has long been associated with female anatomy and therefore used in fertility charms. Comparatively, long turret and tusk shells, as well as coral branches have been used as wards against the evil eye and protecting male fertility.

Mother of pearl buttons and cameos are traditionally made of shell as well, so they can also encapsulate sympathetic magic, while appearing very everyday or normal to others. Similarly, fossil jewelry can be very grounding, yet can pass as an interesting statement piece.

Divination

There are numerous systems of shell-based divination tied to specific spiritual traditions, most famously Yoruba, Santería, Candomblé and Umbanda. If you do not follow those paths, there are other ways to use shells for divination. If you work with runes, you could paint a collection of hardy shells with the symbols. You could craft your own system of "throwing bones" from pieces you find, with the location and time of collection bearing special significance for you. If you like eating clams, that's an easy way to collect and clean a large number of similarly-sized shells. From there you can paint the insides with your own system of symbols and colors.

Altar, Element & Spirit Work

Seashells represent the Element of Water and are used to honor water-based deities and spirits. Larger-sized clam, scallop and abalone shells are handy natural tools for burning, cleansing, and holding. Intact bivalves and snail shells can be made into spirit houses. Fossils on your altar can help connect you with ancient wisdom, the long progression of time, and elements of transformation.

Obtaining Shells & Fossils

If you wish to buy fossils and shells, research the vendor as best you can to make sure they were harvested and collected consciously without harming the environment or impacting endangered species. It's very easy to find pocket guides on shell varieties so you can know more about what you're getting and where they come from.

If you plan on collecting specimens on your own, be respectful: don't damage habitats or collect living samples, and most importantly study up on the local laws before you pick anything up. Some places do not allow you remove anything from a site, so don't be that person.

Study shell specimens closely to make sure it's not alive—snails and hermit crabs are really good at hiding inside their shells. If you're unsure, I find it's best to bring a small bucket with you, fill it with the local water and place the shells in there. After things have settled, watch closely to see if life emerges. If so, release the shell immediately to where you found it.

Lastly, it's a good idea to ask permission of the local spirits before taking anything. If you feel drawn to make an offering in exchange, be sure that it's biodegradable and won't cause any damage to the ecosystem. If you're unsure, taking some extra time to remove trash or debris from a site is also a valid form of exchanging energy and showing your appreciation.

—LAURA TEMPEST ZAKROFF

Witch Windows

WHILE VISITING the state of Vermont in winter, either for a ski break or to see the sugar makers tapping sugar maples (*Acer saccharum*) for their delicious sap, keep an eye out for something unusual in this northern New England state. Though the blazing colors of the autumn foliage have long gone, this fascinating feature of the Green Mountain State is visible year-round.

Typically located in the gable-end wall of a house and rotated approximately 45 degrees from vertical, some windows are hung so that the long edge is parallel to the roof slope. More common in farmhouses from the 19th century, they are found almost exclusively in or near the U.S.

state of Vermont, though some were found as far south as Westborough, Massachusetts. These oddly placed windows were called *Witch Windows* or *Coffin Windows*.

Why Witch Windows?

Why were they called Witch Windows and why were they positioned at such an odd angle? Local folklore posits they were installed to keep Witches from flying into the house. Popular lore held that a Witch in flight would not be able to turn sideways quickly enough to make it through the window. This explanation doesn't make sense, however. Ignoring the fact that Witches don't really physically fly on brooms, why couldn't they turn in time? It's just as impossible as the flying itself. And why couldn't they simply enter through a window hung in the traditional manner?

Coffin Windows

Another tradition holds that the windows were installed to make it easier to remove a body from the upper floors of the house. At face value, this might seem to make sense; after all, in the 19th century in rural Vermont, hospitals were rare, and the custom was for sick and dying individuals to be treated at home. Once again, though, logic slices through this flimsy justification.

The slanted window opened out to a sloped roof. It would be hard and perilous work to push a coffin out this window, catch it from the other side and lower it to the ground. Wouldn't it just be easier for two farmhands to carry the body alone gently down the stairs inside to a coffin waiting on the bottom floor? And why would you carry an empty coffin upstairs to the body in the first place? That means an extra trip.

Lazy Windows

Another name for these slanted windows is *Lazy Windows*. It assumed the person installing the window was just too lazy to measure and frame a new opening. This is closer to the truth than the other beliefs, but the builder was not being lazy. Instead, the worker was being frugal and resourceful. When a house was enlarged by adding to an attic, the space at the gable end—where an opening was needed for light and ventilation—was usually not tall enough for a window to stand upright.

Were They Really There to Prevent Witches?

So now we return to the original question: Why "Witch Windows?" Did people ever really believe they were necessary to prevent Witches from flying in? Probably not. But it made a good story, didn't it? And once told, it was passed on to each young child who asked, "Why is that window like that?"

—MORVEN WESTFIELD

Hocking Hills: A Legend in Stone
Unexpected and Spectacular Rock Formations in Ohio

THE UNLIKELY STORY of the head of a Sphynx peering out of a rock formation near the City of Logan in Eastern Ohio begins over 330 million years ago. At the time the Atlantic Ocean covered that part of what is now the Central United States. When the waters receded, vast deposits of soft sediment, silt, gravel and sand were left behind. The layers settled and formed the black hand stone, as the layered rock which remained is called today. Ten thousand years ago the Wisconsin glacier began to melt. The waters flowed like blood southward, scarring the land. Rushing, the glacial streams cut

and cracked the stone. Overhangs and recessed caves, gorges, rock shelters and water falls were created. In 1924, 146 acres of the incredibly beautiful area was purchased by the State of Ohio and established as Hocking Hills State Park, named for the nearby Hocking River. Hocking derives from the Shawnee language and translates roughly as "bottle neck" or "gourd shaped." This references the curving path of the river bed.

The Devil's Bath Tub as well as the Sphynx, the Rock House, Old Man's Cave, Ash Cave, Pulpit Rock, Cantwell Cliffs and Broken Stairs Falls are a few

of the intriguing and descriptive names given to the giant stone formations. Over the past few hundred years human history has become entwined with the geological history of this unique area. Old Man's Cave is named in honor of one Richard Rowe, a hermit who lived most of his life in the large cave. About 1796 the Rowe family moved from Tennessee to the Ohio River Valley. They planned to open a trading post. Young Richard took his two dogs and continued to travel through Ohio, seeking game. When he found the comfortable cave Richard just stopped and stayed. One cold winter's day he climbed down a gorge for fresh water but forgot his tools. When he tried to crack the ice with the butt of his rifle he forgot to unload it. The gun went off in his face, killing him. His remains were buried at the mouth of the cave. Visitors often claim to be greeted by the hermit's ghost, upon hearing a gun shot and the mournful baying of his hounds, forever waiting for their master to come home. The Old Man's cave actually appealed to earlier occupants. Prior to 1795 the brothers Nathaniel and Pat Rayon built a cabin near the cave's entrance. They are also buried nearby. The Rayon cabin was preserved and was used to dry tobacco for a time. Older artifacts remain in the cave, indicating that Native Americans also lived there.

Ash Cave is named for the huge mounds of ash found there, left by Native Americans for reasons now forgotten. This sandy floored cave echoes with an eerie beauty. The sound is from distant underground waterfalls. Paranormal investigators have identified a number of lingering spirits in Ash Cave. The dance of spectral lights in the surrounding forest at dusk offer further speculation that the area is a portal or vortex open to supernatural forces.

Ghost tours are among the activities offered at Hocking Hills State Park. Other presentations throughout the year include a Maple Syrup Festival, Christmas in Ash Cave, a variety of nature hikes and more.

From Logan, Ohio follow 664 South about 12 miles to visit the park area. It's open daily from 10:00 am–4:00 pm. Tourist cabins, campsites, gift shops and restaurants are nearby. There are hiking trails and kayak and canoe rentals too. The Pencil Sharpener Museum is a stop popular with many park visitors. It displays hundreds of unusual collectible pencil sharpeners.

—ELAINE NEUMEIER

135

the fixed stars

Algol

The Blinking Eye of Medusa

Each year a different fixed star is featured in the astrology section of The Witches' Almanac. This year's choice is Algol, currently located at 26 degrees Taurus 19 minutes. Algol is a rare triple-eclipsing binary star. It has been significant to astrologers for at least 3,200 years when it was included in the Egyptian calendar in the calculation of lucky and unlucky days. Stargazers will be fascinated by watching it blink. Every 69 hours Algol's magnitude will dip for 10 hours. Then it returns to its original brightness, creating a blinking effect in the heavens. The legend is that the blink is really the sinister gaze of the monster Medusa and that this star is the most wicked force in the zodiac. Medusa's hair was hissing snakes and her glance was thought to turn all who looked upon her to stone. Eventually the hero Perseus cut off Medusa's head, nullifying her evil. His sword

hand can be observed holding her slain head in his constellation among the stars.

Algol translates from the Arabic as the Demon Star, Head of the Ogre, Satan's or Specter's Head. In Chinese cosmology Algol is included with a group of negative stars called the Mausoleum. In Hebrew mysticism Algol becomes one of the four different astrological points all named Lilith, a demonic vampire figure, the evil first wife of Adam. All of the astrological Liliths represent the very worst of feminine and lunar energies.

The prominent 17th century astrologer William Lilly gave great credence to Algol, allowing an orb of 5 degrees variance from the exact degree in considering its impact in horoscopes. Usually astrologers use only a small orb of 1 to 3 degrees in interpreting fixed stars. Algol is included among the powerful Behenian stars. The word Behenian translates as "root" from Arabic. There are fifteen stars in this elite classification. They have special sigils and were used in magical workings in the medieval astrology of Europe and Arabia. Behenian stars were held in awe as being sources of planetary power.

Contemporary astrology tends to take a more humanistic and positive approach in interpretation, looking less at celestial forces in terms of absolutes of good and evil and more as energies subject to choices made and free will, at least within limits. Perhaps the secret to finding a redeeming force in the presence of Algol in astrology lies in analyzing the story of Medusa.

Medusa wasn't always evil. Born the only mortal among the three Gorgon sisters, she alone had a beautiful face

and glorious hair rivaling that of the virgin goddess Athena. Athena grew jealous. The great sea-god Neptune saw Medusa walking along the shore and was overwhelmed with passion. Although she tried to resist him, Neptune impregnated Medusa in a temple of Athena. She gave birth to Pegasus and Chrysaor. Enraged, the virgin goddess transformed Medusa's enchanting hair into a coil of serpents making her into a monster.

Channeling the traditional influences of the malefics, Saturn and Mars, combined, Algol has been related to misfortune, violence, unruly mobs, hanging, decapitation and overall mayhem. Unless benefic aspects are present Algol conjunct the Sun or Mars promises a tragic life, being either a victim or perpetrator of crime. Algol with the Moon brings a violent nature and sickness, with Saturn or Neptune tragedy around water. Algol conjunct the Part of Fortune brings poverty, and with Jupiter, injustice, but possible victory in time of war.

Some astrologers claim that with Algol prominent in a birth chart the hair, teeth and facial features will be prominent and unusual. This can be either very beautiful or truly ugly and distorted.

Each year the Sun conjoins Algol on May 15–16. Looking ahead to the coming year Mars will conjoin Algol February 23–27, 2021.

—DIKKI-JO MULLEN

Saying Witch in European Languages

Language	Ways to say Witch
Albanian	magjistare
Basque	sorgina
Bosnian	vještica
Bulgarian	вешица (veshtitsa)
Catalan	bruixa
Croatian	vještica
Czech	čarodějnice
Danish	heks
Dutch	heks
Estonian	nõid

Language	Ways to say Witch
Finnish	noita
French	sorcière
Galician	bruxa
German	hexe
Greek	μάγισσα (mágissa)
Hungarian	boszorkány
Icelandic	norn
Irish	cailleach
Italian	strega
Latvian	ragana

Language	Ways to say Witch
Slovak	čarodejnice
Slovenian	čarovnica
Spanish	bruja
Swedish	häxa
Ukrainian	відьма (vid'ma)
Welsh	wrach
Yiddish	מעכשייפע (mekha sheyfe))

Language	Ways to say Witch
Lithuanian	ragana
Maltese	saħħara
Norwegian	heks
Polish	czarownica
Portuguese	bruxa
Romanian	vrăjitoare
Russian	ведьма (ved'ma)
Serbian	вештица (veshtica)

STEPHEN HAWKING

Looking Through Millions of
Tiny Black Holes at the Theory of Everything

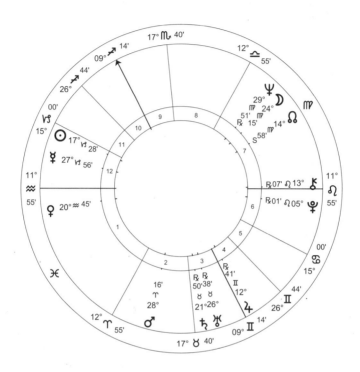

When Dr. Stephen Hawking spoke it was from a wheelchair and through a computerized voice, yet the entire world listened. The renowned British educator and physicist was born on January 8, 1942 in Oxford, England. His 1988 breakthrough publication, "A Brief History Of Time: From The Big Bang Theory To Black Holes" sold more than a million copies, topping the best seller list among nonfiction books for over a year. When asked about his purpose Hawking replied, "My goal is a com-

plete understanding of the universe, why it is as it is and why it exists at all."

Stephen Hawking's birth chart has a wide Sun-Mercury conjunction in Capricorn in the 12th house. This describes his childhood shyness, active inner life and years of increasingly debilitated health. He was stricken with ALS (Lou Gehrig's disease) in 1963. Most of the time a diagnosis with this progressive and incurable condition results in complete paralysis and death within

3 to 5 years. Hawking lived with ALS nearly 55 years. He became a hero and inspiration to disabled people the world over. His natal Pluto in Leo in the 6th house shows the mystery and intensity of his health challenges and describes the masses of people whose lives his illness touched.

As is often the case with a true genius, Stephen Hawking had a difficult time during his early school years. He had a Saturn-Uranus conjunction in Taurus in the 3rd house. He had trouble with most school work, unhappy interactions with his peers and little success at sports. Yet he could immediately grasp problems in math and physics.

Jupiter in Gemini reveals his great curiosity about the structure, origins and space-time relationships of the universe. This Jupiter influence also showed his later academic success. He took first class honors in physics at Oxford University, graduating in 1962 at the age of 20, then went on to pursue post-graduate studies at Cambridge, earning his doctorate in 1966. He occupied the same chair as a professor at the university that Sir Isaac Newton (1644–1727) held. Hawking's talents were recognized and appreciated, and he received encouragement to continue despite his growing health concerns. Jupiter in the 4th house describes a favorable

" Equations are just the boring part of mathematics. I attempt to see things in terms of geometry. "

Stephen Hawking

family heritage too. His father was a successful physician.

Hawking's affinity for computers and the use of technology in order to communicate and continue with his teaching and research is described by the Aquarius ascendant. Venus in the 1st house in Aquarius reveals his charisma. Despite his crippled and nearly immobile body, he was a popular and highly recognizable figure. He traveled a traditional circuit to promote his books in person. The Aquarius influence shows originality and humanistic concerns too. He refused to accept a knighthood, protesting a lack of governmental funding for the sciences.

Hawking once said that marriage gave his life a purpose and the motivation to go on. The North Node, Moon and Neptune form a stellium in Virgo in the 7th house, while Chiron in Leo hovers on the cusp of the 7th. His first wife's care of him and their three children seemed to have been his pillar of strength. Mars in Aries in the 2nd house shows much financial tension. Despite his lifelong connection with Cambridge, the family struggled to pay for his care and other needs for years. Eventually his career became lucrative, as indicated by his grand trine in earth signs, involving the seven placements Capricorn, Taurus and Virgo.

Referencing the work of Albert Einstein (1879 – 1955), Hawking offered a view of the origins of the universe with origins in singularity. He was able to produce current astrophysical data supporting the

$$-\delta\psi_4 + \bar{\delta}\phi_{22} - \Delta\phi_{21} = 3\nu\psi_2 - 2(\gamma + 2\mu)\psi_3$$
$$+ (4\beta - \tau)\psi_4 - 2\nu\phi_{11} - \bar{\nu}\phi_{20} + 2\lambda\phi_{12}$$
$$+ 2(\gamma + \bar{\mu})\phi_{21} + (\bar{\tau} - 2\beta - 2\alpha)\phi_{22} \tag{3.58}$$

$$\delta\phi_{11} - \bar{\delta}\phi_{02} + \Delta\phi_{01} + 3\delta\Lambda = (2\gamma - \mu - 2\bar{\mu})\phi_{01} + \bar{\nu}\phi_{00}$$
$$+ \phi_{10} - 2\tau\phi_{11} + (2\bar{\beta} - 2\alpha - \bar{\tau})\phi_{02} + 3\rho\phi_{12} + \sigma\phi_{21} \tag{3.59}$$

$$\phi_{10} - \bar{\delta}\phi_{01} + \Delta\phi_{00} + 3D\Lambda = (2\gamma - \mu + 2\bar{\gamma} - \bar{\mu})\phi_{00} - 2(\alpha + \bar{\tau})\phi$$
$$2(\bar{\alpha} + \tau)\phi_{10} + 4\rho\phi_{11} + \bar{\sigma}\phi_{02} + \sigma\phi_{20} \tag{3.60}$$

$$-\delta\phi_{21} - \bar{\delta}\phi_{12} + \Delta\phi_{11} + 3\Delta\Lambda = \nu\phi_{01} + \bar{\nu}\phi_{10} - 2(\mu + \bar{\mu})\phi$$
$$+ \lambda\phi_{02} - \bar{\lambda}\phi_{20} + (2\beta - \tau)\phi_{12} + (2\bar{\beta} - \bar{\tau})\phi_{21}$$
$$+ 2\rho\phi_{22} \tag{3.61}$$

beginning of matter concentrated in a single dense point. The most familiar singularity involves the nature of millions of black holes forming after an original big bang, about 20 billion years ago marking the origin of the universe. In the 1980's Hawking answered Einstein's famous and unanswered unified field theory. This explains the four major interactions addressed in modern physics.

With his six retrograde planets as well as the Part of Fortune in Libra in the 8th house, an esoteric interpretation of Hawking's birth chart would point to karmic patterns coming into play, with past life and futuristic impacts related to his discoveries. It is interesting that Hawking passed away at age 77 on Albert Einstein's birthday, March 14, 2018.

Professor Stephen Hawking left a number of famous quotes about aliens and the universe for us to ponder. Here are two in honor of this witty and enigmatic genius. He also warned that overpopulation and artificial intelligence pose the greatest threat to human life in the future.

1. "I believe alien life is quite common in the universe, although intelligent life is less so. Some say it has yet to appear on planet Earth."

2. Look up at the stars and down at your feet. Try to make sense of what you see, and wonder about what makes the universe exist. Be curious."

—DIKKI-JO MULLEN

STEPHEN WILLIAM HAWKING
Born January 8, 1942
At 10:26 AM (War Time) Oxford, England

Data Table
Tropical Placidus Houses

Sun 17 Capricorn 29—12th house

Moon 24 Virgo 15' — 7th house (waning Moon in the disseminating phase)

Mercury 27 Capricorn 56—12th house

Venus 20 Aquarius 46—1st house

Mars 28 Aries 17—2nd house

Jupiter 12 Gemini 41—4th house (retrograde)

Saturn 21 Taurus 50—3rd house (retrograde)

Uranus 26 Taurus 39—3rd house (retrograde)

Neptune 29 Virgo 52—7th house (retrograde)

Pluto 5 Leo 01—6th house (retrograde)

N. Moon Node 14 Virgo 58—7th house

Chiron 13 Leo 08—7th house (retrograde)

Part of Fortune 18 Libra 42—8th house

Ascendant (rising sign) is 11 Aquarius 56

CELESTIAL POWERS

Lightning Gods, Bolts from the Blue

FROM ANCIENT TIMES and ancient places, the Supreme Deity controlled the sky. People tended to call them thunder Gods rather than lightning Gods, but thunder is only bluster. Lightning is the boss and its power manifests in formidable numbers. A bolt can travel at the speed of 130,000 mph and reach a temperature of 54,000 degrees F. In its area, lightning immediately sizzles the air to 36,000 degrees F, about three times hotter than the surface of the Sun. This sudden intensity constricts the clear air, producing a supersonic shock wave sliding acoustically into the boom of thunder that sends pets and sometimes people hiding under beds.

Since sound fails to lend itself to image, "Thunder Gods" are depicted with lightning bolts. The zigzag icon serves as the main attribute of Zeus, for instance, along with the eagle and the scepter. In 265 BCE Theocritus writes of the Greek Deity, "Sometimes Zeus is clear, sometimes he rains." The name of Zeus, supreme ruler of Mount Olympus, derives from *dios*, "bright," and he is also known as Zeus Astrapios, "lightbringer."

The Romans know a wondrous pantheon when they find it. When Zeus emerges as Jupiter, the newborn sky God assumes the same attributes. Jupiter too has a bolt to hurl, an eagle, a scepter and even more weather nomenclature. Known as Dios Pater, Shining Father, he is also worshipped as Jupiter Elicius (weather, storms), Jupiter Fulgurator (lightning), Jupiter Lucetius (lightning), Jupiter Pluvius (rain).

Thor, the Norse weather deity, has his own lightning icon made by dwarves — the hammer Mjollnir, "that smashes." When Thor throws the hammer, lightning flashes. Then Mjollnir returns like a boomerang to his right hand, on which Thor wears an iron glove. Sometimes the red-bearded giant blasts lightning bolts from the eyes, adding to his ferocious appearance. The Norse believe that Thor creates thunder when he rumbles through the sky on a carriage pulled by two goats, Tanngrisnir (Gap Tooth) and Tanngnostr (Tooth Grinder).

Our early forefathers believed that the most powerful of Gods control the weather, weather controls fertility and fertility controls survival.

Power cult, lesser known

Perkons prevails as a Pagan weather God less known to us, but widely venerated throughout the old Baltic pantheon. In Latvia, Lithuania, Prussia, and sometimes Russia, the deity turns up in powerful fertility rites as agriculture begins to put down roots. The cult continues until twelfth-century restrictions, sometimes underground, and pockets of practice may still be found in the region. A Catholic clergyman, D. Fabricius, writes in 1610: "During a drought, when there has not been rain, they worship Perkons in thick forests on hills and sacrifice to him a black calf, a black goat and a black cock. When the animals are killed, then, according their custom, the people come together from all the vicinity, to eat and drink there together. They pay homage to Perkons by first pouring him beer, which is first brought around the fire, and at last pour it in this fire, asking Perkons to give them rain."

The God's whole family helps with his work, resonating farming tradition skyward. The sons strike lightning and

thunder, the mother and daughters send rain, and the daughter-in-law peals thunder to rival the deity's own ear-cracking level. The Perkons cult appeals to him in folk songs. One peasant sings to bring rain because "the shoots of barley are faded," while another lyric gives thanks for the autumn harvest.

The Heavenly Wedding

Beyond the rustic, Perkons offers more complexity. He is also depicted bristling with weapons, a "silver rider on a golden horse," the answer to an old riddle. He bears a sword, an iron rod, a golden whip, a fiery club, a gun, a knife. Among the arms he always carries a "thunder ball," which helps to create lightning, thunder and mastery of the Devil. Many of the God's followers wear on their clothing small axes as adornments. The axe amulets represent thunder balls—symbols of symbols—believed to heal illnesses.

Legends abound, sometimes centering on food. Perkons drowns Baba because she has violated a ritual by giving him spoiled food. In another story a foe holds out bread and butter, concealing a knife in the other hand. Folk belief has it that setting out food for the God calms storms and that honeycombs thrown into a fire dispels clouds.

In the Heavenly Wedding tale, Perkons rides off to bless an event of mythological splendor—the marriage of the Moon, Menulis, to Saule, daughter of the Sun. On his way Perkons stops to strike an oak tree, his own attribute; the twisted roots are a favorite hiding place of the Devil. In Latvian folklore especially, the evil spirit is depicted as stupid, taunting, easily tricked and

Perkons' prime adversary. Once his tree is rid of the evil spirit, the fertility God proceeds to the wedding and sanctifies bride and bridegroom.

As for the marriage, however blessed, an old Latvian ballad shuns any "happily ever after" whipped cream on the wedding cake:

In the first blush of Spring Saule and
　　Menulis married.
Saule rose early, leaving
　　Menulis's side.
Menulis went out on his own.
Menulis made love to Ausrine.
Perku-nas, with great anger,
Struck Menulis with his sword.
"Why did you leave Saule?
Why did you make love to Ausrine?
Why did you wander about in
　　the dark?"

The song explains why the Sun shines during the day and the Moon shines at night, according to fabled belief—he there, she here, she there, he here. Although apart, they both desire to sojourn below and share beloved Daughter Earth.

—BARBARA STACY

The Beasts of Borges

IN 1957 JORGE LUIS BORGES, the superb Argentinian poet, published the *Manual de zoología fantástica*. A later English edition, the *Book of Imaginary Beings*, created with translator Norman Thomas di Giovanni, contains descriptions of 120 mythical beasts from folklore and literature. There follow some of our favorites.

In the preface, Borges states that the book is to be read "as with all miscellanies not straight through. Rather we would like the reader to dip into the pages at random, just as one plays with the shifting patterns of a kaleidoscope."

Á Bao A Qu—A creature that lives on the staircase of the Tower of Victory in Chitor. It may only move when a traveler climbs the staircase, and it follows close at the person's heels. Its form becomes more complete the closer it gets to the terrace at the tower's top. It can only achieve this ultimate form if the traveler has obtained Nirvana, otherwise it finds itself unable to continue.

Animals in the Form of Spheres—At the time of its writing, some believed that planets and stars were actually living beings, and that the movement of the heavenly bodies was voluntary.

Antelopes with Six Legs—According to Siberian myth, these six-legged antelopes were far too fast for human beings to catch. A divine huntsman, Tunk poj, cut off the animal's rearmost legs to make the animal easier for humans to hunt.

The Ass with Three Legs—This massive creature is said to stand in the middle of the ocean. It has three legs, six eyes, nine mouths, and one golden horn.

Bahamut—A huge, measureless fish which is often used to describe the spaces between Heaven, Earth, and Hell.

Catoblepas—Described as a black buffalo with a hog's head, this creature's head is so heavy that it constantly hangs low to the ground. It is also believed that, like the basilisk, looking into its eyes will kill you instantly.

Celestial Stag—No one has ever seen a Celestial Stag. They live in underground mines, searching for the light of day. They will attempt to bribe, speak to, and even torture miners in their quest to reach the surface, where they turn into a deadly liquid form.

The Chinese Fox—These foxes appear like average foxes, but may sometimes be seen standing on their hind legs to walk. They presumably live about a thousand years, and are bad omens for their mischievous ways. They are known to shapeshift and are able to see into the future.

Eater of the Dead—Most commonly associated with Egyptian myth, the Eater attends to the "wicked." It is described as having the head of a crocodile, the midsection of a lion, and the hindquarters of a hippo.

Eight Forked Serpent—A massive serpent with eight heads and eight tails. Its eyes are a deep red, and trees are said to grow along its back.

The Elephant that Foretold the Birth of the Buddha—A white elephant with six tusks that appeared in a dream to, as its namesake suggests, foretell the birth of Buddha.

The Wonders of God's Creation Manifested in the Variety of Eight—A mysterious creature that lives in the world of Bliss. Allegedly, all sounds, sights, and smells to this creature are divine.

Fastitocalon—A massive whale that many sailors often mistake for an island.

Fauna of Mirrors—It was believed that another world existed behind all mirrors, inhabited by a wide amount of unknown and strange creatures. Luckily, our worlds are now cut off from one another.

Gillygaloo—A bird which nests on mountain slopes and lays square eggs, which lumberjacks use as dice.

Goofang—A fish ("about the size of a sunfish but much bigger") which swims backwards to keep the water out of its eyes.

Goofus Bird—A bird that builds its nest upside down and flies backwards.

Huallepen—A swift moving dog with a human head, which laughs maliciously.

Hundred Heads—The Hundred Heads was said to be a gigantic fish with many heads, each one that of a different animal. Legend holds that the fish was the reincarnated spirit of a monk who had often called others "monkey head" or something similar. The karma of these insults had made him return as a monster.

The Lamed Wufniks—There are precisely thirty six Lamed Wufniks in existence. It is said that, without knowing it, they support the universe and affirm God. If one comes to realize their purpose, they immediately die and are replaced by another unsuspecting man.

Lamia—Half woman and half serpent, these creatures are said to have sprung from one of Zeus's varied love interests. They are thought to be sorceresses, and although they cannot speak they whistle sweetly.

The Leveler—Reputed to live on the planet Neptune, this creature is ten times the size of an elephant, and looks quite a bit like it. Its most remarkable features are its conical legs (which are flat on the bottom). Bricklayers employ the Leveler to flatten hilly areas for construction projects. It is herbivorous and has few enemies.

The Monkey of the Inkpot—An extract from Wang Tai Hai describes a small creature with black fur and scarlet eyes that sits by writers and drinks their leftover ink.

The Mother of Tortoises—A giant tortoise made of water and fire, on whose shell is written the "Universal Rule," a divine treatise.

Ping Feng—A black pig with a head at each end.

Pinnacle Grouse—Has only one wing, and flies in a continuous circle around the top of a mountain.

Strong Toad—Distinguished from other toads by its turtle like shell, the Strong Toad glows like a firefly, cannot be killed except by burning, and can attract or repel anyone nearby with its stare.

Swedenborg's Angels — Perfected souls of the blessed and wise, living in a Heaven of ideal things, each reflecting the perfection of this realm.

Swedenborg's Devils—These are people which, after dying, choose to go to Hell rather than to Heaven. They are not happy there, but they are reputed to be more content in hell than they would have been in heaven.

The T'ao T'ieh—A dog with one (often monstrous) head attached to two bodies, which symbolizes the sins of gluttony and greed.

—BARBARA STACY

150

The Heron

A Heron was walking sedately along the bank of a stream, his eyes on the clear water, and his long neck and pointed bill ready to snap up a likely morsel for his breakfast. The clear water swarmed with fish, but Master Heron was hard to please that morning.

"No small fry for me," he said. "Such scanty fare is not fit for a Heron."

Now a fine young Perch swam near.

"No indeed," said the Heron. "I wouldn't even trouble to open my beak for anything like that!"

As the sun rose, the fish left the shallow water near the shore and swam below into the cool depths toward the middle. The Heron saw no more fish, and very glad was he at last to breakfast on a tiny Snail.

Moral: Do not be too hard to suit or you may have to be content with the worst or with nothing at all

LEAD

•

CURSE

•

TABLETS

dEUO
NOdENTI SILUIANUS
ANILUM PEPdEdIT
dEMEdIAM PAPTEM
dONAUIT NOdENTI
INTEP 9UIbUS NOMEN
SENICIANI NOLLIS
PETMITTAS SANITA
TEM dONEC PEPFEPA
US9UE TEMPLUM
dENTIS

EVIDENCE OF THE ROMAN influence on Britain is still apparent today. They introduced a water system, built straight roads and created major cities such as London (Londinium). They also left behind numerous artifacts including a type of votive offering called a curse tablet.

Curse tablets are small metal sheets or slabs with a curse or request of favor from the Gods inscribed upon them. The curses or requests fall into five general categories: litigation, competition, trade, erotic concerns and prayers for justice.

Many of the curse tablets found in Great Britain called upon the Gods to punish thieves. Others asked the Gods to influence the outcome of a court trial or prevent an opponent for speaking against the supplicant.

Gamblers asked for fortune to favor them in games of chance, wrestling or chariot races. Others requested a different kind of "win": that of the heart of a would-be lover.

Materials

Curse tablets can be made from any non-perishable material, but they were most often made from lead, tin, stone or baked clay. One curse from Bath was written on a pewter plate. The durability of the material, plus the practice of burying the tablets in secret places, assured that the curse would remain intact for a long time.

Lead or a lead/tin mixture was chosen most often. It can be pounded into thin sheets and is soft enough to scratch with a fingernail, making it ideal for engraving. It lasts hundreds or thousands of years. Leaden pipes from Roman times still carry water in some European cities. And it was available—the Romans were the first to exploit lead on an industrial scale.

It also has compatible magickal properties. Governed by Saturn, the ruler of the dark, it promotes contact with deep unconscious levels. Although Saturn is also associated with protection and defensive magic, he is more well known as the "stern taskmaster," one who teaches a hard lesson. How appropriate for a curse tablet asking for punishment of theft!

Writing and Language

Though some tablets were marked with only a series of scratches or not marked at all, typically the text of the curse was scratched (written) in cursive script running from left to right or right to left. The text could also be written bi-directionally in a format known as boustrophedon. Meaning "turning like oxen in ploughing," text written in boustrophedon format reverses at the beginning of a new line.

That is, if the text is written as left-to-right (as English is), at the end of

the line, the writer turned the tablet 90 degrees so that the would be inscribing in the other direction, upside-down. Another variation was to write single letters backward or to change the word order. These departures from normal writing were possibly meant to give a sense of mystery or to confuse an unauthorized reader if someone found the tablet.

An aggrieved person might hire a professional scribe to write the curse tablet, allowing a common petitioner more choice in language and format. While most texts from Roman Britain were written in Latin, they were also written in Greek or the Celtic language known as Brittonic. This language was spoken by the inhabitants of Britain before the Roman conquest.

The Curse

Once cast, curses were irrevocable unless the Gods or the petitioner repealed the curse.

Most curse tablets followed a strict formula. Tablets started with the invocation of a deity, spirit or mythological creature. Petitioners praised deities in flowery language such as "Good and beautiful Proserpina," or merely addressed the deity by name ("Lord Neptune").

Petitioners seeking vengeance might beseech Gods or spirits associated with the Underworld such as Pluto. They might invoke a local God instead of one of the major Roman Gods if the petitioner felt a specific link to that deity or if a specific deity was linked to the place where the malfeasance occurred. In 1979-1980, a team of archaeologists discovered around 130 tablets during an excavation of the Roman Baths and Temple at the city of Bath in England. Most concerned the theft of clothes while the victim was bathing there. Sulis Minerva, to whom the Temple was dedicated, was often the deity petitioned.

Then came the naming. Sometimes the person uttering the curse was named, though often he or she was not, in order to prevent counter curses. Then the person who was to be cursed was named. If the name perpetrator wasn't known, the petitioner would describe the wrongdoing ("the person who has stolen my bathing tunic and cloak" or "the man who has taken my wife").

The curse then laid out the punishment to be levied. In severe cases, a petitioner might ask for death, but for theft and other petty crimes, more likely they asked for disruption of bodily functions (eating, sleeping, urinating, defecating) or for ill health (fevers, general malaise) until the petition was answered. For theft, the term of the punishment was usually until the goods were returned.

The following is an example from one tablet. Solinus is the petitioner, the thief's identity is not known and Sulis Minerva is the Goddess who is appealed to for help.

"Solinus to the Goddess Sulis Minerva. I give to your divinity and majesty [my] bathing tunic and cloak. Do not allow sleep or health to him who has done me wrong, whether man or woman or whether slave or free unless he reveals himself and brings those goods to your temple."

It was also customary to include a promise of offerings to the Gods such as dates, figs or pigs as a payment for their services.

Fixing the Curse

The final step for a pliable lead or lead/tin sheet was to roll or fold the tablet with the text facing inward and "fix" the curse with an iron nail. This fixing is responsible for the Latin name for the tablets, *tabella defixionis*, or defixio: meaning "to pin down."

When finished, the tablet was left in a place associated with the deity. Tablets whose text invoked Gods of the Underworld were often left at graves or thrown into wells, the better to be closer to the realm of those Gods. Sacred pools at temples were another common place. Petitions to Sulis were plentiful at Bath.

Other Uses of Curse Tablets

Tablets used for romantic or erotic love often called upon Venus (or the Greek equivalent, Aphrodite) for aid. The petitioner could be male or female and the relationship to the person they desired could be heterosexual or homosexual. The aid requested could be to attract another or to break the bond between the one you desired and an existing partner. Tablets were placed in water (to connect with seafoam-born Aphrodite) or inside the home of the desired target.

Spells to gain advantage in court or in the political arena make up the litigation category. Associated with Jupiter, tin is used ritually for success in business and in legal matters. Therefore it's the magickally preferred material for these tablets, either alone or in combination with lead.

Curse tablets were also used for competitions. Those used to thwart a rival charioteer could be violent, often asking the Gods to wreck the chariot, causing severe injury or death to driver and horse alike. Less violent ones might ask the Gods to prevent the horses or charioteers from doing their best. One example from the 3rd century asks the Gods to "Bind the horses whose names and images on this implement I entrust to you" and "bind their [charioteers'] hands, take away their victory." These tablets were often affixed to posts in the area where the races were held.

Curse Tablets Today

So what's stopping one from making curse tablets today? Ethics, for one thing. Cursing, especially cursing to death, is generally considered wrong, though some paths allow it under certain dire circumstances and others under any circumstance. Before you consider creating a curse tablet, consider your path, your ethics and your motives. Also consider whether there is another, less drastic way to achieve your goals than cursing. Instead of asking the Gods to make a thief suffer with fever until he returns a stolen item, ask the Gods to make the person suffer guilt (but only if this is within your ethical bounds).

If you decide to use a curse tablet, say, as a prayer to ask for retribution of a wrong ("prayer for justice") or success in a court of law, consider your material. Though you can buy lead sheets from a building supply company, do you want to? Lead is poisonous. It enters the body through inhalation of lead dust or through accidental ingestion via contaminated hands, clothing and surfaces. Tin, which is not poisonous to handle, is available in sheets, resists weathering, resists corrosion and is associated magickally with success. (Just be careful with the sharp edges.) Or use a piece of clay pottery, painting the text on the surface instead of inscribing it.

Finally, promise a "payment" that does not require animal sacrifice. Promise the God or Goddess fresh flowers on the altar, a new statue, a new altar cloth, volunteer work or donation to a charity.

—MORVEN WESTFIELD

Moon Cycles

A New Moon rises with the Sun,
Her waxing half at midday shows,
The Full Moon climbs at sunset hour,
And waning half the midnight knows.

NEW	2021	FULL	NEW	2022	FULL
Jan 13		Jan 28	Jan. 2		Jan. 17
Feb 11		Feb 27	Feb. 1		Feb. 16
Mar 13		Mar 28	Mar. 2		Mar. 18
Apr 11		Apr 26	Apr. 1		Apr. 16
May 11		May 26	Apr. 30*		May 16
Jun 10		Jun 24	May 30		June 14
July 9		July 23	June 28		July 13
Aug 8		Aug 22	July 28		Aug. 11
Sept 6		Sept 20	Aug. 27		Sept. 10
Oct 6		Oct 20	Sept. 25		Oct. 9
Nov 4		Nov 19	Oct. 25		Nov. 8
Dec 4		Dec 18	Nov. 23		Dec. 7
			Dec. 23		

*A rare second New Moon in a single month is called a "Black Moon.".

Life takes on added dimension when you match your activities to the waxing and waning of the Moon. Observe the sequence of her phases to learn the wisdom of constant change within complete certainty.

Dates are for Eastern Standard and Daylight Time.

presage

by Dikki-Jo Mullen

ARIES, 2020 – PISCES, 2021

Every twenty years or so astrology's Great Conjunction occurs. This astrological pattern correlates with profound events which reshape history. The Great Conjunction is the conjoining of Jupiter and Saturn, the two celestial heavyweights in the solar system. On December 21, 2020 at 6:22 pm, GMT, the Great Conjunction will be exact at 0 degrees Aquarius 29 minutes. The last Great Conjunction took place in the year 2000. History fans might recall how this twenty-year interval has marked major milestones in the human condition. For 140 years or so the Great Conjunction takes place in the same element. Then it mutates. 2020 marks a switch from conjoining in earth signs to air signs. This promises a new twist on world affairs for decades to come.

What might we expect? Well, this powerful Jupiter-Saturn conjunction last took place in Aquarius 600 years ago. That's when the Ming Dynasty established Beijing as the capital of China.

At the same time the Ottomans were engaged in a seven-year struggle for the throne of Wallachia, the historic region of Romania. That ended in the formation of the Prussian Federation. Against the cyclical background of time, the Great Conjunction in Aquarius promises new values and new types of government. Out of chaos can emerge a completely different world. Economic values and ecology should be affected as both are ruled by Earth, the outgoing element. One thing is certain, the year ahead will be interesting.

As you explore what all of this means to you, start with the forecast for your Sun sign. Next, consider the forecast for your Moon sign, which addresses emotional needs and responses. Finally, turn to the forecast for your rising sign, the ascendant, for insight concerning your physical presence, as you interact with the people and places around you. Those born on a cusp may consult both forecasts. Discover more about all of this in Presage.

ASTROLOGICAL KEYS

Signs of the Zodiac
Channels of Expression

ARIES: fiery, pioneering, competitive
TAURUS: earthy, stable, practical
GEMINI: dual, lively, versatile
CANCER: protective, traditional
LEO: dramatic, flamboyant, warm
VIRGO: conscientious, analytical
LIBRA: refined, fair, sociable
SCORPIO: intense, secretive, ambitious
SAGITTARIUS: friendly, expansive
CAPRICORN: cautious, materialistic
AQUARIUS: inquisitive, unpredictable
PISCES: responsive, dependent, fanciful

Elements

FIRE: Aries, Leo, Sagittarius
EARTH: Taurus, Virgo, Capricorn
AIR: Gemini, Libra, Aquarius
WATER: Cancer, Scorpio, Pisces

Qualities

CARDINAL	FIXED	MUTABLE
Aries	Taurus	Gemini
Cancer	Leo	Virgo
Libra	Scorpio	Sagittarius
Capricorn	Aquarius	Pisces

CARDINAL signs mark the beginning of each new season — active.
FIXED signs represent the season at its height — steadfast.
MUTABLE signs herald a change of season — variable.

Celestial Bodies
Generating Energy of the Cosmos

Sun: birth sign, ego, identity
Moon: emotions, memories, personality
Mercury: communication, intellect, skills
Venus: love, pleasures, the fine arts
Mars: energy, challenges, sports
Jupiter: expansion, religion, happiness
Saturn: responsibility, maturity, realities
Uranus: originality, science, progress
Neptune: dreams, illusions, inspiration
Pluto: rebirth, renewal, resources

Glossary of Aspects

Conjunction: two planets within the same sign or less than 10 degrees apart, favorable or unfavorable according to the nature of the planets.

Sextile: a pleasant, harmonious aspect occurring when two planets are two signs or 60 degrees apart.

Square: a major negative effect resulting when planets are three signs from one another or 90 degrees apart.

Trine: planets four signs or 120 degrees apart, forming a positive and favorable influence.

Quincunx: planets are 150 degrees or about 5 signs apart. The hand of fate is at work and unique challenges can develop. Sometimes a karmic situation emerges.

Opposition: a six-sign or 180° separation of planets generating positive or negative forces depending on the planets involved.

The Houses — *Twelve Areas of Life*

1st house: appearance, image, identity
2nd house: money, possessions, tools
3rd house: communications, siblings
4th house: family, domesticity, security
5th house: romance, creativity, children
6th house: daily routine, service, health
7th house: marriage, partnerships, union
8th house: passion, death, rebirth, soul
9th house: travel, philosophy, education
10th house: fame, achievement, mastery
11th house: goals, friends, high hopes
12th house: sacrifice, solitude, privacy

Eclipses

Elements of surprise, odd weather patterns, change and growth are linked to eclipses. Those with a birthday within three days of an eclipse can expect some shifts in the status quo. There will be five eclipses this year, four are partial and one is total.

June 5, 2020 – Full Moon – partial lunar eclipse in Sagittarius, South Node

June 21, 2020 – New Moon- partial solar eclipse in Cancer, North Node

July 5, 2020 – Full Moon – partial lunar eclipse in Capricorn, South Node

November 30, 2020 - Full Moon - partial lunar eclipse in Gemini, North Node

December 14, 2020 - New Moon- total solar eclipse in Sagittarius, South Node

A total eclipse is more influential than a partial. The eclipses conjunct the Moon's North Node are thought to be more favorable than those conjunct the South Node.

Retrograde Planetary Motion

Retrogrades promise a change of pace, different paths and perspectives.

Mercury Retrograde

Impacts technology, travel and communication. Those who have been out of touch return. Revise, review and tread familiar paths. Affected: Gemini and Virgo

June 18–July 12, 2020
in Cancer

October 14–November 4, 2020 in Libra and Scorpio

January 30, 2021–February 21, 2021
in Aquarius

Venus Retrograde

Venus retrograde influences art, finances, and love. Affected: Taurus and Libra

May 13–June 25, 2020
in Gemini

Mars Retrograde

The military, sports, and heavy industry are impacted. Affected: Aries and Scorpio

September 10–November 14, 2020
in Aries.

Jupiter Retrograde

Large animals, speculation, education, and religion are impacted. Affected: Sagittarius and Pisces

May 14–September 13, 2020
in Capricorn

Saturn Retrograde

Elderly people, the disadvantaged, employment and natural resources are linked to Saturn. Affected: Capricorn and Aquarius

May 11–September 29, 2020
in Capricorn and Aquarius.

Uranus Retrograde

Inventions, science, electronics, revolutionaries and extreme weather relate to Uranus retrograde. Affected: Aquarius

August 15, 2020–January 14, 2021
in Taurus

Neptune Retrograde

Water, aquatic creatures, chemicals, spiritual forces and psychic phenomena are impacted by this retrograde. Affected: Pisces

June 23–November 29, 2020
in Pisces

Pluto Retrograde

Ecology, espionage, birth and death rates, nuclear power and mysteries relate to Pluto retrograde. Affected: Scorpio

April 25–October 4, 2020
in Capricorn

ARIES
March 20–April 19
Spring 2020–Spring 2021 for those
born under the sign of the Ram

Aries embodies the spirit of springtime. An impulsive and competitive pioneer, the energetic Ram keeps going and growing. Challenges and adversity fuel the motivation to explore limits and transcend boundaries. Easily bored or distracted, Aries can burn out. Making a habit of fulfilling promises and completing projects is important. Otherwise actual accomplishments can fall short of goals.

Mars, your ruler, highlights career goals during early spring. The Aries New Moon on March 24 reveals the specifics regarding opportunities. April 11–27 Mercury races through your sign. Journeys are rewarding. Dedicate May Eve to a prosperity rite. Financial prospects are a focus during May. Explore suggestions about generating extra income. Retrograde Venus and the Sun stir your sector of variety and communication in June. Diplomacy is essential in both business and personal conversation. Multitasking provides refreshing breaks in the daily grind.

At the Summer Solstice the solar eclipse affects family life, a trend continuing through mid-July. Address housing issues. Uphold family traditions. Visitors arrive during late July. Plan a house party with a home-cooked meal to celebrate Lammastide.

Fiery transits of Mars, the Sun and Mercury heighten your vitality during the first three weeks of August. You are in your element enjoying recreation and vacation travel. The New Moon on August 18 celebrates the accomplishments of loved ones. Late August shifts the focus to maintaining wellness. Honor your body with healthy dietary and lifestyle choices, including plenty of rest. The Full Moon on September 2 joins Neptune in your 12th house. Dreams offers spiritual guidance. The weeks before the Autumnal Equinox will find you unusually introspective and quiet. September 23–October 2 brings a Venus-Mars pattern which encourages artistry. Create beauty with handicrafts or appreciate art and music.

Avoid adversaries during early to mid-October. An opposition from retrograde Mars to your 7th house can revive an old grudge or stoke a rivalry. The New Moon on October 16 reveals the specifics. It's best to focus on future goals and avoid those who upset or anger you. As All Hallows approaches, your sector of mystery and the spirit world is activated. Omens bring comforting messages from those who have passed away. A traditional ghost costume would be a good choice for Halloween parties. November 1–13 oppositions from Mercury and Venus find others making plans for you. Cooperate. Team efforts lighten the work load and offer camaraderie. On the 14th Mars completes its retrograde in your 1st house. You will easily assume a position of leadership, taking charge of situations by the end of the month. The lunar eclipse on November

30 is very stimulating mentally. Enroll in a class, visit a library or bookstore. Participate in a discussion group.

On December 1, Mercury joins the Sun in your 9th house. Curiosity about foreign customs, spiritual topics and animal communication occupies your thoughts during the weeks before the Winter Solstice. On December 15 a favorable Venus transit begins. Shop for holiday gifts and finery. Deck the halls. The remainder of December promises much revelry as well as financial gain.

January 1–7 will be hectic. A Mercury-Mars pattern can make you unintentionally abrupt. Be sensitive to others. January 8–19 a Venus-Sun transit makes you highly visible, especially among professional contacts. You are a rising star in a career setting. January 20–31 the Sun, Saturn and Jupiter cluster in your sector of goals and friendships. You can become more involved in an organization and dedicate time to worthwhile causes. At Candlemas recite affirmations by candlelight. Plan for the times ahead. Mercury affects your social circle during the first three weeks of February. Longtime acquaintances can be in touch. Patterns repeat, for better or worse. Choose helpful people and worthy projects. Past experiences reveal what the future will bring. The Full Moon on February 27 focuses on following a wholesome diet and daily activity schedule.

As March begins a Venus influence deepens concerns for those in need. A thoughtful deed brings inner peace. On March 4 Mars changes signs. Through the rest winter new ideas and surroundings are explored. Brainstorm. Intriguing opinions are exchanged.

HEALTH

Mars transits Aries from late June until January 6. You will be attracted to fitness programs and maybe extreme sports. Pace yourself, rest as needed and much progress toward health-related goals can be achieved. During the eclipse pattern June 5–July 5 drink plenty of fluids. Protect yourself from the Sun with dark glasses, hats and sunscreen.

LOVE

Your romantic attractions are fiery, frequently beginning suddenly and ending explosively. Involvements can be turbulent during the spring and autumn. The New Moon on August 18 favors your love sector, bringing a change for the better. A friend can either become a lover or introduce you to a special someone when Jupiter brightens your section of wishes from December 23 through the remainder of winter.

SPIRITUALITY

Tiger's eye agate (to achieve desires and winning the battle of life) and lodestone (for strength of character) are stones to wear or carry to heighten spiritual energies. The total solar eclipse on December 14 in your sector of the higher mind promises profound spiritual realizations near the Winter Solstice.

FINANCE

Venus, ruler of your money sector, is retrograde during May and June. Conserve and avoid risks during that time. Lucky Jupiter crosses your midheaven from spring until December 18, promising rewards and recognition leading to greater security.

TAURUS
April 20–May 20
Spring 2020–Spring 2021 for those
born under the sign of the Bull

Luxurious surroundings and predictable days are preferred by this peaceful, Venus-ruled Earth sign. There is an affinity with nature and a sensitivity to sound. Many Taureans are talented musicians or gardeners. Determined Taureans firmly hold on to what they have while acquiring even more of what they want.

Spring begins with a burst of energy regarding professional aspirations. Mars is strong throughout March and April. Competitive situations and controversy keep things interesting. Respond to volatile people with humor and patience. The New Moon on April 22 promises a fresh start.

Dedicate a charm for travel on May Eve. Mercury and the Sun are in your 1st house through May 11. This promises an interest in exploring new places and new ideas. Mid-May finds Venus turning retrograde in your financial sector, a trend lasting until June 25. Conserve on expenses and be patient if seeking a pay raise. The eclipse on June 5 brings revelations about how the decisions of others are affecting your own financial security. Managing investments and financial settlements are concerns through the Summer Solstice. On the longest of days express gratitude.

From the end of June until July 12 retrograde Mercury creates a stir in your 3rd house. Allow for delays in commuter travel. A vehicle might need maintenance or a route might change. Relationships with neighbors and relatives assume an unpredictable quality. Clear communication helps. By the end of July financial matters look better. Supportive aspects involving Venus in your money sector develop. Dedicate Lammas to addressing your financial needs and honoring your career situation. During the last three weeks of August your 3rd house of communication is augmented. You will charm and impress others with your pleasant conversation. August 20 through the beginning of September is favorable for vacation travel. At the Full Moon on September 2 involvement in community life increases. Interesting new people enter your social circle.

September 6–26 Mercury points to your health sector. You will seek ways to make your daily environment more healing and wholesome. A special new animal companion, a potential familiar, may join your household near the Autumnal Equinox. October finds Venus crossing into your romance and pleasure sector. Love, new hobbies and recreational pursuits make life as bright as October's beautiful autumn foliage. October 23–31 accents the success of a partner. All Hallows coincides with the Blue Moon in Taurus. Invitations and costume suggestions contributed by others make this Halloween a serendipitous and delightful celebration.

Questions of balance and correctness arise as November opens. Your focus shifts toward the need to blend personal wishes with the roles others play in your life. On November 14 Mars changes direction in your 12th house. Old grudges and resentments are released. This results in greater inner peace as the month ends. The eclipse on November 30 favorably influences financial opportunities. You are entering a cycle of enhanced prosperity. On December 1 a stellium of planets begins to form in your 8th house. The finances of those closest to you, joint assets and investments, are of significance. The December 14 eclipse reveals a long buried secret. You discover something new about the life of a loved one who is no longer with us. By December 19 Jupiter crosses your midheaven where it will remain for nearly a year. This points to your potential and expertise being recognized. An impending promotion or other promising opportunity is possible. At the Winter Solstice celebrate new possibilities, nurture self confidence.

January 1–6 a Mercury-Mars square makes you overly vocal. Avoid heated verbal exchanges with those who might disagree with you. On January 7 Mars enters your sign where it remains until March 3. A cycle of growth begins. You will be ready to make changes. From mid-January until Candlemas a positive Venus transit in your 9th house brings satisfaction through enjoying the arts as well as other cultural topics. A congenial in-law or grandparent - grandchild relationship brightens the deep winter days. Bless the family bond by burning multicolored candles on your altar. Fixed sign transits are especially influential during February. Habits and customs are supported by many. Others can seem overly set in their ways. Strike out on your own; be self-sufficient and independent.

March ushers in greater cooperation and a more unified spirit. The New Moon on March 13 introduces worthwhile aspirations which manifest during the last weeks of winter.

HEALTH
The Full Moon on April 7 brings in a month-long cycle of insights regarding health needs. Control that sweet tooth. A solar transit through your health zone September 22–October 22 points to healing and better vitality.

LOVE
The planetary love goddess, Venus, welcomes the Spring Equinox in your birth sign. March 20–April 2 favors making a true love connection. During October your love light again shines brightly. A soul mate waits nearby at the Full Blue Moon in Taurus on Halloween, October 31.

SPIRITUALITY
The moss agate (connects with the Earth) and chrysocolla (honors the divine mother) are your spirit stones. Saturn hovers in your 9th house of spirituality March 22–December 16. This assures practical and realistic support through spiritual realizations.

FINANCE
Financial decisions made during the summer develop into profitable situations throughout the remainder of the year. Jupiter trines your Sun until December 18. This fortunate aspect indicates overall monetary gains.

GEMINI
May 21 – June 20
Spring 2020 – Spring 2021 for those born under the sign of the Twins

The complex Twins communicate a constant flow of ideas. Life is fueled by curiosity and the quest for knowledge. There are so many variables that the inconsistent path is maze-like and the pace is quick. Rest is seldom a priority when there is much life to be lived and so much to see and do. There is an axiom among astrologers that if one doesn't like a Gemini, just wait a bit. He or she will turn into someone else.

At the Spring Equinox Mercury and Neptune aspect your Sun. Sift through facts to dispel any confusion and analyze options. A symbolic dream brings insights regarding an important project by April 2. On April 3 Venus begins a two-month transit through your sign. Your creative output accelerates. The Full Moon on April 7 is in your sector of love and pleasure. It reveals the specifics of the best choices to make through May Eve. May 1 – 10 Mercury and the Sun are in your 12th house. You will cherish your privacy. Satisfaction is found in rescuing a person or animal companion in need. Keep secrets.

Venus turns retrograde in May in your sector of physical appearance. Take extra care with grooming and remember to use good manners throughout May and June. Prepare to make a good impression as your birthday month approaches. The eclipse on June 5 points to shifting alliances. A legal matter might need attention.

The Summer Solstice brings an eclipse in your money sector. Prepare a rite to attract prosperity. Be receptive to changing financial trends. New sources of income might become available as the summer begins. On July 12 Mercury completes its retrograde and solutions to cash flow concerns emerge. Conversations offer valuable guidance through Lammastide. August 5 – 17 finds you multitasking. Visit a bookstore or library to enjoy new publications near the New Moon on August 18. August 20 – September 9 planetary transits prioritize home and family concerns. A move might be considered. Visitors can arrive at your residence. Mars turns retrograde on September 10 in your 11th house of wishes and social contacts. New goals emerge. The days preceding the Autumnal Equinox favor tactfully releasing troubled or needy individuals. Making wise choices is the key to success near the Full Moon on October 1.

Venus transits your 4th house of family concerns October 3 – 27. A relationship with a relative improves. Complete any repairs needed to your dwelling. Decorate your residence for the autumn holidays with colorful gourds, Indian corn and foliage. As the Full Moon on October 31 approaches, images of past lives manifest. Assemble a costume honoring a previous incarnation.

November 1 – 10 centers on your zone of hobbies and pleasure. Plan enjoyable activities to make the most of leisure time. November 11 – 29 finds the Sun and

Mercury joined by Venus in your wellness sector. Healing from physical or emotional ills begins. An animal companion is nurturing. The lunar eclipse in Gemini on November 30 offers insight into your personal strengths and weaknesses. Look at the Full Moon and reflect on words of the ancient Oracle of Delphi, "Know thyself."

December opens with an important focus on relationships. Others make plans and have expectations. The total solar eclipse underscores the specifics. A commitment can change as the Winter Solstice nears. Jupiter enters your 9th house of higher thought and philosophical concerns on December 19 where it will remain throughout the winter. Pursue higher education travel opportunities. Late December is a wonderful time for writing. What about that book you have in your head?

Venus joins the Sun and Pluto in your 8th house during the last three weeks of January. Insurance or tax concerns can be effectively addressed. The financial situations of others impact your own. Retrograde Mercury begins on January 30. It favorably aspects your Sun until February 21. At Candlemas reread your journal or Book of Shadows by candlelight. Recall the patterns in your life, whether they are good or not. Experience is a wonderful teacher during February. On February 25 Venus crosses your midheaven. A friend can assist you in reaching a goal. Remember social niceties. On March 4 Mars enters Gemini where it will remain through the winter. Your energy level intensifies; you are motivated to move forward. The last days of winter crackle with excitement. Time passes quickly.

HEALTH

Pluto, ruler of your health sector, is retrograde April 26–October 5. Past health habits will be reflected in current wellness concerns then. Focus on purging toxins from your body and environment. At the eclipse on November 30 simplify your life. Clearing away clutter would encourage well-being.

LOVE

Venus makes an exceptionally long transit through Gemini this year, from April 3 to August 6. Romantic bliss will definitely be on the upswing during that time. An old flame might rekindle while Venus is retrograde May 13–June 25. The eclipse on December 14 in your sector of partnership can augur a change regarding marital status.

SPIRITUALITY

Both Jupiter and Saturn enter your 9th house of spiritual awakening near the Winter Solstice. Yuletide celebrations will offer unique and powerful spiritual insights. Rhodochrosite (the rainbow bridge stone of transition) and agates (for strength and versatility) are helpful stones suitable to wear or carry to heighten spirituality.

FINANCE

The June 20 eclipse at the Summer Solstice creates a stir in your money sector. There can be shift in employment status near then. The Full Moon on December 29 also affects security issues. Your insight into finances deepens as winter begins.

CANCER
June 21 – July 22
Spring 2020– Spring 2021 for those
born under the sign of the Crab

Reserved and sensitive, the Crab will dwell happily in homey and protected surroundings. Memories and keepsakes are treasured. The past forever colors the present and future in the hearts and minds of these gentle, Moon-ruled souls. The whole world can feel like family to empathetic Cancerians. Special attachments are often formed with the very young and the elderly.

From the Spring Equinox through March 30 transiting Mars, Jupiter and Pluto oppose your Sun. Others just don't see eye to eye with you. Detachment and compromise might be the most appropriate way to cope. March 31– April 13 a genteel Mercury-Neptune pattern soothes hurt feelings. A dream or intuitive hunch provides guidance and perspective. The last half of April accents your 8th house of research and mysteries. Insight concerning financial planning as well as rapport with the spirit world develop. On May Eve add a bouquet of spring blossoms to the altar to honor departed loved ones. The Full Moon on May 7 brightens your sector of romance and creativity. Accept invitations and enjoy hobbies during the remainder of the month.

June finds Venus transiting your 12th house. Volunteer work for a worthwhile charity can be satisfying. You will long to help those in need. The June 21 eclipse in Cancer shifts your focus in a new direction. At the Summer Solstice consult the Tarot or tea leaves for guidance. It's time to move on. Late June through July 12 Mercury is retrograde in your 1st house. Vintage attire and visits to places of historic significance can be appealing. A friend or relative who has been out of touch contacts you near your birthday. A strong Mars influence intensifies through Lammastide. This makes you rather impatient. Focus on stress release, perhaps including soothing music and meditation in the ritual celebration.

August 7– September 5 Venus glides through your birth sign. It's an ideal time to plan a vacation or to socialize. An important relationship moves in a positive direction. September 6– 26 Mercury affects your sector of home and family. Your thoughts are focused on living arrangements and understanding relatives. A family meeting would offer valuable insights. At the Autumnal Equinox perform a house blessing or Feng Shui to clear any discordant energies in preparation for the new season.

The two Full Moons in October, on the 1 and 31, shift your focus to career goals, politics and networking. A variety of projects appeal to you. On the 14th Mercury turns retrograde. The pre-Halloween season assumes a nostalgic and sentimental quality. Plan a traditional ritual honoring All Hallows with an ancestor altar. Offer a libation of hot mulled cider. November 1–20 cardinal sign transits encourage independence. As November ends, the health of both the mind and body is a focus. The eclipse on

November 30 accents both mental and physical health.

A bright Venus transit brings positive social events December 1–13. A party or musical or theatrical presentation would be especially memorable. The eclipse on December 14 may bring unexpected changes in your daily schedule. Be flexible regarding Winter Solstice celebrations. Animal companions add to the magic of the longest of nights. At the end of December, Jupiter and Saturn cross the cusp of your 8th house. Omens and synchronicities suggest messages from the spirit world.

Be tactful in communication from January 1–6. An intense Mercury-Mars square can instigate an unfortunate argument. On January 7 Mars changes signs and moves to sextile your Sun. Goodwill is restored. A supportive friendship grows closer by Candlemas. Bless relationships of all kinds with silver and gold tapers at a ritual gathering.

February brings a stellium of planets into your 8th house. Financial planning is important. Study how investments and shared assets affect your personal monetary needs near the New Moon on February 11. After retrograde Mercury is over on February 21 business situations stabilize. February ends with the Sun joining Neptune in your 9th house sparking a quest for philosophical insights. Visit a sacred site or pursue spiritual studies. Mars enters your 12th house as winter ends, generating an introspective mood. You will cherish times of quiet reflection.

HEALTH

The lunar eclipse on June 5 brings insight regarding health. Be aware of any changes in your vitality then. The circulation in the lower limbs might benefit from elevating or massaging the legs. Mars will square your Sun June 28–January 6. This can be a time when pressures build and it can be hard to relax. Moderate exercise and stress release can help.

LOVE

The Full Moons on May 7 and December 29 promise new love connections. Visit the seashore or lakefront while Venus is in Cancer August 7–September 5. At that time a current relationship can deepen or an interesting new person might enter your orbit.

SPIRITUALITY

Neptune is in the midst of a long transit through your 9th house of spiritual awareness. Attune to spiritual nuances by recording and interpreting dreams. Draw down the Full Moon on September 2 for a lasting spiritual awakening. Your spirit stones are quartz (for clarity and direction) and moonstone (heightens intuition and attunes to the Moon).

FINANCE

Oppositions from Saturn and Pluto caution you about blindly following the advice of others. Trust your own instincts on financial management. This is especially true near the time of the eclipse on July 5. From mid-January on, previous efforts are rewarded and financial gains can be expected.

LEO
July 23–August 22
Spring 2020–Spring 2021 for those
born under the sign of the Lion

Bright and vibrant as a sunny morning, the Lion of the zodiac is both playful and majestic. An inherent nobility and enthusiasm combined with a knack for making the best of things propels Leo into a position of leadership. Generous and dramatic with a charming self confidence, Leos celebrate life in a manner that can seem grandiose to some, but lovable overall. Creative ability, dignity and an appreciation for quality will usually characterize those born under this vibrant fire sign.

Unpredictable Uranus is crossing your midheaven, along with Venus at the Vernal Equinox. There can be some shifting loyalties and other changes brewing at work. Adapt, be flexible. In ritual use a chant to enhance insight. A friend offers heartfelt advice March 20–31. April begins with Mars moving into an opposition aspect, a trend which remains until mid-May. There is a competitive spirit; someone can be critical or challenging. Maintain cordiality. Significant information arrives the week of the Full Moon on April 7. On May Eve offer tokens of goodwill and at least one difficult person will become an ally. May 12–28 Mercury joins Venus in your sector of long-term goals and social contacts. You will exchange ideas about

choices for the future. Involvement in an organization can interest you. At the lunar eclipse on June 5 a loved one's needs and requests take precedence.

As the Summer Solstice nears, you will become more introspective. Quiet reflection can help you to release that which isn't serving you. On June 28 Mars shifts into a fire sign and begins to favorably aspect your Sun. Your energy level will improve. A journey or study program, perhaps involving a foreign language or spiritual topic, can spark your enthusiasm during July. By Lammastide, Saturn is retrograde in your health sector. Consider having a healing circle at the seasonal ritual. Serve fresh fruit or juices afterward to follow up on the healing theme. August 5–19 Mercury speeds through your birth sign, accenting travel and communication. Your eloquent words attract a worthwhile opportunity. Celebrate your birthday with an outing during this time. The New Moon in Leo on August 18 is a fortunate time to write a wish list to aid in manifesting all you desire during the coming year. Late August–September 5 transits in your 2nd house favor financial planning. Consider taking on extra work to earn additional income.

September 6–October 2 Venus transits Leo. Pursue a favorite hobby or sport. A cherished relationship brings deep happiness at the Autumnal Equinox. Honor unity at a ritual observance. The Halloween season finds Mars retrograde in your 9th house of higher consciousness. You might reexamine spiritual beliefs and explore the tenets of your childhood faith. An in-law, grandparent or grandchild can need your encouragement to overcome an obstacle. At All Hallows favorite literary characters inspire costume ideas. Throughout the first three weeks of November Venus favors your 3rd house. Pleasant messages are exchanged. This is also a good time for journaling or creative writing, perhaps poetry. On November 22 there is a shift toward 5th house matters which lasts through mid-December. Love connections intensify. Plan some pre-Yuletide projects with a loved one, such as decking the halls, baking cookies or shopping for gifts.

January 1–6 Venus and Mars both trine your Sun. A spiritual question or ethical dilemma is resolved. Life moves forward. From early January to March 3 Mars joins Uranus in your 10th house. Both planets will square your Sun. You are ready to end a troublesome association or dead-end project. The Full Moon in Leo on January 28 brings a focus on what is truly significant. Celebrate Candlemas in early February with a purification rite. Decorate an all white altar, include a single white rose in a crystal vase surrounded by white votive candles. At the New Moon on February 11 a partner makes significant announcement. Late February–March 12 a Mercury, Jupiter and Saturn transit in your 7th house. This emphasizes the choices, needs and decisions of importance to others. Cooperation and compromising will help you to accomplish what matters most. At the New Moon on March 13 emphasis shifts to your sector of mysteries. A puzzle is solved. Research undercovers hidden truths as winter ends.

HEALTH

Saturn transits your 6th house of health July 2–December 18. Select healthy diet and lifestyle choices then to lay the foundation for wellness in the future. A turning point regarding a health concern is reached near September 29 when Saturn turns direct. Overall your health should improve during the autumn months.

LOVE

The June 5 and December 14 eclipses focus on your love sector, marking important developments regarding affairs of the heart. During the last three weeks of September a Venus passage through Leo favors romantic connections. Prepare a love talisman at the Autumnal Equinox.

SPIRITUALITY

Neptune is in the midst of a transit through your 8th house, suggesting connections with spirit entities. The Full Moons on September 2 and October 1 are favorable times to explore philosophical concepts, meditation and spiritual topics. Your spirit stones include amber (to release anger and stress) and sunstone (for health and attracting success).

FINANCE

Mercury rules your cash flow and earning powers. Conversations and studies relating to finance can often assist with monetary matters. Retrograde Mercury cycles usually offer insights about repeating patterns regarding finances. Be wary of acting upon risky advice or loaning money when Jupiter opposes your Sun during the winter months.

VIRGO

August 23–September 22

Spring 2020–Spring 2021 for those
born under the sign of the Virgin

The most efficient use of time is a priority for this particular and dedicated earth sign. Virgo revels in bringing order out of chaos. Wholesomeness, nutritious food choices and worthwhile activities will appeal to those born under this conscientious, Mercury-ruled sign. Meaningful goals, productive studies and travel all are priorities.

Springtime begins with Mars in an energetic aspect in your 5th house of romance and leisure. March 20–30 finds you engrossed in an enjoyable activity, perhaps involving a hobby, with a loved one. March 31–April 10 Mercury and Neptune oppose you. There can be some mixed messages and confusion in communication. Verify plans and clarify agreements to keep matters running smoothly. In April Venus begins a long transit through your career sector. Incorporate creativity and social activities with work to increase your income.

On May Eve prepare an eloquent description or a bit of poetry to share at a seasonal gathering. This will delight others. The Sun and Mercury favor your 9th house in the first half of May, supporting educational goals and travel. A conversation with in-laws or other relatives provides valuable insights. At mid-month both Saturn and Venus turn retrograde. There can be a backlog of work to complete. A strong Mars aspect commences on May 13. Challenges and a competitive mood make life interesting yet complex through the Summer Solstice. The eclipse on June 5 focuses on changes affecting family life. A residential move or home improvement project can be considered.

Retrograde Mercury June 18–July 12 in your sector of social contacts brings news from longtime friends. Enjoy an eventful visit near the Summer Solstice. Preserve memories of the occasion on film. Your 11th house of wishes is the focal point of strong cardinal sign transits July 13–21. Delays or unreliable people might test your patience. The New Moon on July 20 finds you anxious to move forward. A Mercury-Saturn opposition near Lammas suggests someone seeking a helping hand. Respond by incorporating a healing circle into the usual holiday rites. By August 7 Venus impacts your social life, promising cheerful companionship. An affectionate, creative and/or well-to-do person becomes a bigger part of your life during mid to late August. In early September follow through with travel opportunities. After September 10, when Mars turns retrograde in your 8th house, there may be a need to evaluate joint finances or investments. A previous experience repeats regarding a business partnership. Express gratitude at the Autumnal Equinox for the resources and blessings you've been given.

Throughout most of October Venus transits Virgo, activating your 1st house. Others will be favorably impressed by you. Both love and money situations are favored. Mercury is retrograde at Halloween. Resurrect a favorite costume making sure that it's easy to wear. November 1–9 there is an emphasis on your 2nd house. Keep up with new developments affecting your salable job skills. To do so, consider attending a conference or reading current publications. Mid-November highlights your 3rd house of travel and communication. Prepare to make a series of short commutes. Respond to messages promptly. The eclipse on November 30 opens new career opportunities.

December 1–20 the focus is on hearth and home. The December 14 eclipse brings a new slant on holiday revelries. At the Winter Solstice a friendly ghost from Christmas past visits. December 29–January 6 Mercury and the Sun activate your sector of leisure and love. Play a game or share a hobby with the one you care deeply about. On January 7 Mars enters your 9th house where it will remain until early March. Your motivation perks up. Write about an interesting journey or spiritual insight. January 8–31 a cheerful Venus trine supports nurturing new social contacts and savoring beauty. Attend a cultural event such as an art opening, ballet or the theatre. At Candlemas Mercury is retrograde in your 6th house. Meditate by candlelight for insights about health.

On February 27 the Virgo Full Moon is powerfully aspected by 7th house oppositions. Seek to understand the spiritual perceptions influencing others. A discussion can clear away confusion. By March 4 Mars crosses your midheaven. Companions appreciate your leadership. Your conscientious efforts win you respect during the last days of winter

HEALTH

Uranus rules your health sector. New technologies and innovative wellness trends intrigue you and are worth exploring. Uranus trines your Sun all year, suggesting freedom from major health concerns. Since earth signs are involved, spend time outdoors absorbing the healing influences of nature.

LOVE

Jupiter blesses your romance sector from the Vernal Equinox until the Winter Solstice. A love connection grows and deepens. Near the July 5 eclipse a loved one shares a tender sentiment. A romantic surprise is planned.

SPIRITUALITY

With Neptune in your 7th house all year, a partner profoundly influences your spirituality. Full Moon observances on September 2 and February 27 promise spiritual awakening. Apatite (for manifestation and self expression) and fluorite (for clarity of thought) are stones to connect with for spiritual renewal.

FINANCE

Venus rules your 2nd house of income. Analyze your past financial patterns while Venus is retrograde May 13–June 25 for insight. A favorable Jupiter transit from the Vernal Equinox through December 18 points to financial gain.

LIBRA
September 23–October 23

Spring 2020–Spring 2021 for those
born under the sign of the Scales

This Venus-ruled sign is all about part-nerships, love and peace. Harmony and pleasantries are sought, yet dis-cussions of opposing views are wel-comed. Libra seeks balance, forever preferring to avoid extremes by drift-ing too far or doing too much in any one direction.

Dedicate the Vernal Equinox rites to blessings, wellness. Mercury tran-sits your health sector until April 10. Be well informed about health. Venus begins a long transit through your 9th house from early April until August 6. Connections made during journeys can enhance both business and personal aspirations. This influence favors cre-ative writing and study.

May Day finds Mars favorably influ-encing your Sun, an energizing trend which remains until May 12. Dance among the flowers to honor the sabbat. On May 13 Venus turns retrograde, until June 25. Be tolerant if any social situa-tions turn awkward. Budget carefully. June finds Mars stirring your 6th house. Your daily routine becomes especially busy. Animal companions can offer stress release, but may also need extra TLC. The eclipse on June 5 finds you multitasking; mail or messages require timely attention.

You face career options at the Summer Solstice. The solar eclipse is exactly on your midheaven. You will be highly vis-ible. Burn silver and gold candles during the seasonal observance to attract glory and appreciation.

Angular cardinal sign transits during July bring an urge to act upon situations immediately. There is an undertone of impatience. The eclipse on July 5 impacts home and family life. A house-hold repair or the needs of a relative are highlighted. At Lammastide, Sun and Mars influences shine on long-term goals. Visualize what you want at the holiday. Try affirmations to aid mani-festation. The New Moon on August 18 is progressive. Clarify your direction. In late August, Mars and Pluto are at odds; your 4th and 7th houses are hot spots. Maintain happiness in a close relation-ship by taking steps to make home life more comfortable and peaceful.

September begins on an introspec-tive note. You might retreat to read or meditate until the 5th. Mercury races through your sign September 5–26. Follow through with travel opportuni-ties. You will gain in knowledge and experience this month. At the Autumnal Equinox, a favorable Venus influence encourages group participation in sea-sonal observances. The Full Moon on October 1 deepens your bond with a close partner. Others make plans and offer suggestion. A memorable birth-day celebration might be arranged. Mercury is retrograde in your financial sector in mid to late October. Repay a loan or debt. Ingrained financial pat-terns are creating your monetary situa-tion. Venus enters Libra as All Hallows nears. New friendships deepen. Others cultivate your company. Employ your natural artistry to create an original Halloween costume. Include some beads, glitter and crystal accents.

During November, Mercury, Mars and Neptune turn direct. A confusing situation involving a relationship or legal matter is resolved. Consider a natural or alternative remedy to address a health concern. The eclipse on November 30 ushers in a spiritual awakening. Venus blesses your 2nd house of cash flow during the first half of December. Financial gain is promised. On December 19 lucky Jupiter enters your 5th house of love and pleasure. Plan a winter holiday with a loved one. The longest of nights evokes a happy, cozy mood.

January 1–7 brings a potent Mercury influence to your 4th house. Listen to relatives. Visitors might arrive at your home. Mars transits your 8th house from January 7 through winter's end, bringing insights about the afterlife. A medium can verify a message from the spirit world. By Candlemas Mercury is retrograde in your 5th house. Complete craft projects to share at a holiday get-together. Mid-February–March 15 brings a winning combination of Mercury-Jupiter influences to favorably aspect your Sun. Insights concerning the pursuit of happiness materialize. March 1–19 Venus joins Neptune in your 6th house. Trust your intuition concerning animal communication. You will experience deep psychic attunement. This assists in connecting with both plants and animals as winter wanes.

HEALTH

Flushing toxins from the body by drinking plenty of fresh water can enhance well-being. Your kidneys and lower back area tend to be vulnerable. Symbolic messages in dreams bring health insights at the Full Moon on September 2 and again in early to mid-March.

LOVE

Maintain the status quo regarding your relationship status while Venus is retrograde May 13–June 25. Stay hitched if in a relationship, but if single remain footloose and fancy-free then. The Full Moon in Libra on April 7 and good Venus transits during late October to mid-November and again the first half of February promise happy love connections.

SPIRITUALITY

Stones to enhance your spiritual energies include labradorite (for attunement with extra terrestrial beings, also balances the kidneys) and tourmaline (for avoiding and neutralizing negative energies). Higher spiritual awareness arises during the Yuletide season this year, starting with the total eclipse on December 14.

FINANCE

Pluto rules your financial sector. Be aware of how you can best apply worldwide economic trends to your own situation. Real estate transactions or a home-based business can be especially profitable for you from springtime through the Winter Solstice.

SCORPIO

October 24–November 21

Spring 2020–Spring 2021 for those
born under the sign of the Scorpion

The quest for discovering what is truly
meaningful inspires the Scorpion. The full
scope of life is experienced by confronting
fears and rising above them. This especially applies to the fear of death. Scorpio
seeks to be fully engaged in worthwhile
activity. This Pluto and Mars-ruled water
sign expresses things in extremes. Feelings
range from pure love to loathing. Courage
combined with a sense of purpose creates
exceptional survival skills.

The Vernal Equinox finds Mercury
gliding through your 5th house of
love until April 10. Discuss plans and
ideas with a loved one. Travel can be
involved. In mid-April Mars impacts
your section of family life and residence.
There might be a conflict among relatives
to settle. A mystery can be involved. The
New Moon on April 22 focuses on the
future direction of a partnership. Pluto
turns retrograde just before May Eve.
Plan a traditional May Queen observance, including a maypole dance.

The Scorpio Full Moon on May 7
highlights ecology. Deepen your connection with the Earth. Plant a garden
or enjoy an outdoor walk at moon-
rise. Earth elementals, the gnomes and
brownies, are afoot. In mid-May Venus
turns retrograde in your 8th house

of financial planning. Review insurance coverages. Make needed budget
changes before the Summer Solstice.
Midsummers Day brings an eclipse in
your 9th house. Travel to destinations
offering educational or mystical experiences would be worth exploring as
summer begins. July 1–12 Mercury
completes its retrograde. Old mis-
understandings involving in-laws or
grandparent/grandchild issues can be
resolved amicably. Late July through
Lammastide strong Mars influences
can bring exposure to extreme weather
or challenging sports. Get enough rest
balanced with gentle exercise. August
5–20 Mercury and the Sun will tag
your midheaven. Professional aspirations will be a focus. You will be highly
visible at work and could try a new project or position. Late August through
September 5 a favorable Venus aspect
brings pleasure through imported cui-
sine and cultural influences from afar.
Cultivate friendships with those from
diverse backgrounds.

During mid-September, Mercury
transits your 12th house of solitude
and reverie. You will tend to retreat.
Bless and assist those less fortunate
at the Autumnal Equinox. Engaging
in charitable work would be healing
and satisfying as the new season commences. In October, Mercury, Neptune
and Mars are retrograde, turning your
focus toward the past. Don't allow
yourself to feel haunted by old regrets
or choices that can't be changed. Put
memories to rest at the New Moon
on October 16. Look toward present and future prospects instead. The
Full Moon on All Hallows heightens

your sensitivity to sound and color. Collect a cornucopia of gourds and colored leaves and enjoy music which embodies the spirit of the holiday. In November health issues can improve as both of your celestial rulers, Mars and Pluto, turn direct. Mercury transits Scorpio, November 11–December 1, bringing sharp insights which help you to make the best choices.

Venus blesses you with a conjunction to your Sun during the first half of December. Accept holiday invitations and plan your own pre-Yuletide gathering. The eclipse on December 14 reveals what is most valuable. Offer homemade gifts and treats to save money while surprising loved ones. Jupiter enters your 4th house of home and family life just before the Winter Solstice. Open the windows on the shortest of days to release stale energy. Perform a house blessing. Share spiritual insights at the Full Moon on December 29. Connections with those closest to you deepen as the month ends.

January 1–6 a Venus influence brightens the financial situation. Mars is in your zone of partnerships January 7–March 3. Others are more assertive, suggesting plans involving you. Cooperation leads to progress. Mid-January emphasizes your 3rd house, indicating travel, new ideas and multitasking. The New Moon on January 13 clarifies the specifics. Venus, the Sun and retrograde Mercury brighten your home environment at Candlemas. A quiet, comfortable holiday observance at your own hearth would be enjoyable. Promising love trends enhance your life from February 25 through the end of the winter. Venus conjoins Neptune in your love sector, pointing to a soulmate connection. The New Moon on March 13 reveals more details.

HEALTH
Mars makes a long transit through your health sector from late June to early January. This provides an energy boost, but also can heighten stress. Pace yourself with demanding work or exercise. Health goals can be achieved this year.

LOVE
Intuitive Neptune is in the midst of a long passage in your love sector. Sleep on it. Try lucid dreaming or dream interpretation to discover true love. August, December and March bring encouraging influences for love from Venus.

SPIRITUALITY
The eclipse on June 21 points to sudden and life-changing spiritual experiences during the summer months. The Blue Moon on October 31 brings serendipitous events which also promise spiritual awakening. Stones to wear or carry to enhance spirituality include petrified wood (aids in past life recall) and bloodstone (guards health).

FINANCE
Eclipses this year on June 5 and December 14 create cosmic fireworks in your 2nd house of cash flow. New ways of earning money can replace established resources. Flexibility is your key to making this a profitable year. September–early December is a promising time for adding to savings.

SAGITTARIUS
November 22–December 21

Spring 2020–Spring 2021 for those
born under the sign of the Archer

A free-spirited adventurer, the Archer embraces excitement. Cultivating a zest for life is your motivation. Customs and precedence are often flouted by Sagittarius, the zodiac's nomad. The sky above is wide and expansive and the path ahead is a twisting and unpredictable one. Animal companions, wild and domestic, will usually accompany those born under this Jupiter-ruled fire sign.

The Vernal Equinox brings a Mars-Jupiter conjunction in your money sector. Through the end of March, effort poured into financial goals will bring progress. April begins with Venus crossing the cusp of your 7th house of relationships. You are charmed by a charismatic and talented associate. The Full Moon on April 7 clarifies goals and favors networking. Prepare a charm of herbs and crystals for health on May Day. May 1–11 Mercury activates your 6th house of health. Thoughts and conversations will revolve around maintaining wellness. During the last half of May through June 27 a Mars influence upon home and family life can make home maintenance or the needs of relatives a concern. The Summer Solstice marks a time of endings. Release brings peace and reveals options for the future.

During early July financial management is important. After July 12, when Mercury turns direct, you can feel more settled regarding money and security issues. At Lammastide fire sign transits favorably aspect your Sun. Add a fire source, candles or incense, to your altar. The 2nd and 3rd weeks of August illuminate your 9th house. Plans for travel or a study program are coming together. New prospects interest you. The New Moon on August 18 is a time to commit and choose.

Late August–early September your midheaven is prominent. Career aspirations are important. Pursue a promotion or new professional challenges. On September 13 Jupiter, your ruler, turns direct. Financial gains are likely through the autumn months. Your past efforts are about to be rewarded. The Autumnal Equinox highlights your 11th house of social consciousness. You might be drawn into community service. Support a worthwhile cause. October 3–27 Venus shifts to your 10th house of fame and fortune. Friends support your path to success. Try creative ideas, perhaps involving the arts, to enhance your work.

At All Hallows a furtive, secretive mood prevails. Be subtle and patient. Take time out for solitary contemplation on Halloween. A plain, all-black costume would be suitable. A karmic situation unfolds from the end of October through early November. The New Moon on November 15 brings closure to this cycle. Mars turns direct in your 5th house of love and pleasure during mid-November. You can make progress in sports and other leisure time pursuits. A love connection is moving forward too. Neptune turns direct on November 29 and the Full Oak Moon sheds light on the truth at the lunar eclipse on November 30. This regards a partnership or legal issue.

Your birthday promises to be memorable this year. A total eclipse in Sagittarius on December 14 brings a shift in the status quo. Accept change and growth and all will be well. Jupiter enters your 3rd house near the Winter Solstice. Variety and novelty will be appealing throughout the winter season. Consider taking a short journey or go visiting at the holiday. Read seasonal poetry by the light of a bayberry candle on the longest of nights. December 15–January 7 Venus transits Sagittarius, your 1st house. Much love surrounds you. Wear new clothing, try a different hair style, etc. This helps to make a great impression now, attracting much that is good.

On January 7 Mars joins Uranus in your 6th house, a trend which remains through March 3. It's time to get organized. The winter days bring a rather hectic but interesting daily schedule. Hit the reset button at the New Moon on January 13. The Full Moon on January 28 accents spiritual perspectives and stimulates an interest in new subjects. Visit a favorite bookstore or library; purchase some reading material. Discuss the insights you discover at a Candlemas circle. Mid-February features a multi-planet stellium in your 3rd house. A neighbor or sibling suggests pursuing a worthwhile project or travel opportunities. In March the Sun, Mercury and Venus highlight home life. Consider redecorating. As winter ends prepare home-cooked meals. Invite family or friends to share.

HEALTH

Two eclipses, the partial lunar one on June 5 and the total solar one on December 14 are in your 1st house. Keep your environment comfortable and wholesome. Dressing comfortably will make you feel good. Taking extra care with your appearance at work and play this year will have the added benefit of supporting good health.

LOVE

Passionate Mars transits your 5th house of romance June 28–January 6. An intense attraction develops. Keep this positive though. Move on if a situation turns difficult, angry or compulsive; especially when Mars is retrograde September 10–November 14. Yuletide brings a Venus influence which promises a happy twist to love.

SPIRITUALITY

The eclipse on June 21 highlights your 8th house, enhancing connections with the spirit world while deepening mystical awareness. The summer season favors attending a séance. Your spirit stones are jasper (guards freedom and independence) and turquoise (attracts wealth and love).

FINANCE

Jupiter remains in your 2nd house of cash flow from the Vernal Equinox until December 18. This is very favorable for finances overall. The July 5 eclipse is a time to reconsider any risky financial choices. Be careful not to overextend during the summer months or in late winter.

CAPRICORN

December 22 – January 19

Spring 2020 – Spring 2021 for those
born under the sign of the Goat

With a disciplined practicality Capricorn steadily builds a lasting foundation for a productive life. Integrity and a solid respect for quality is present. Seeking the most practical use of time and assets to create the best personal domain appears to be a rather serious business. Underneath hovers a surprise. There is humor present and a willingness to extend a helping hand to the deserving.

Spring welcomes you with tremendous enthusiasm and energy. The Vernal Equinox finds Mars conjoining your Sun through the end of March. You will be motivated to both work and play hard. April 1–9 Mercury and Neptune blend with your 3rd house. Your insight is good. New ideas are suggested in conversations enabling you to make wise choices. Your 4th house of home and heritage is highlighted April 10–22. Time spent at home is enjoyable and nurturing. Late April through mid-May your 5th house of pleasure is in the spotlight. On May Eve prepare a love sachet of fragrant flowers. Focus on a promising romance or enjoying a favorite game.

The last half of May favors getting organized and tying up loose ends as Saturn will be retrograde. Others express valuable suggestions in June. Listen carefully. Transiting Mercury impacts your relationship sector. The eclipse on June 21 reveals the future of a commitment. At the Summer Solstice share a ritual observance to bless valuable personal connections. The July 5 Capricorn eclipse in your 1st house brings surprising personal insights. Heed a déjà vu from July 1–12 while both Mercury and Saturn are retrograde. The long, warm late July days bring growth through reflection on previous experiences.

Honor Lammastide with a traditional observance. Share whole grain bread and salt at a seasonal feast table. The first three weeks of August emphasize your 8th house of mysteries and the spirit realm. The New Moon on August 18 brings a sense of peace and comfort regarding past life memories. Honor one who has passed away. Late August–September 5 Venus brightens your 7th house of close relationships. A partner's success brings you happiness. Your ties to others, whether business or personal, are positive. Mars turns retrograde in mid-September, affecting your heritage and residence. A nostalgic mood prevails. Relatives who have been out of touch might visit or contact you. At the Autumnal Equinox, decorate the altar with heirloom tableware and linens. On September 29 Saturn turns direct in Capricorn, your 1st house. Personal plans for the future are a focus. Your sense of purpose intensifies as October begins.

October 3–27 Venus favorably aspects Jupiter, Saturn and Pluto, benefitting your 9th house. Travel to sites of spiritual and historic interest; consider higher education or writing for publication. At All Hallows, Mercury affects your career sector, a pattern lasting until November 10. Focus ritual work on blessing your career path. Bring some seasonal magic into your workplace using Halloween, Day of the Dead or Thanksgiving decorations. Late November to mid-December brings the need for extra rest and time for reverie. You will feel more introspective and be more reserved than usual. This solitary mood peaks at the time of the total eclipse on December 14. At the Winter Solstice Mercury enters Capricorn, where it remains until January 7. This brings a burst of mental energy and some travel possibilities. Many plans for the future are considered as your birthday nears.

Venus conjoins your Sun January 8–31. Life is quite good. Your efforts bring financial rewards and friendships are supportive. A love connection is promising. Near the New Moon on January 13 the good times are in full swing. Candlemas brings a potent grouping of planets, including Jupiter and Saturn, in your 2nd house of cash flow. Ignite green and gold tapers after sunset, adding a prosperity affirmation. Financial goals are within reach after Mercury turns direct on February 21. Late February–March 3 a Mars influence in your 5th house finds you preparing for leisure time activities. You will be successful in encouraging children during this time also.

Prioritize at the end of March. Mutable sign transits affect your 3rd house. It's easy to get distracted. As winter ends, your words carry a unique magic. Diplomacy attracts opportunities.

HEALTH

Venus transits your health sector April 4–August 6. This can make rich, high calorie foods, especially sweets, very appealing. Enjoy them, but keep portions controlled to maintain optimum weight. The eclipse on November 30 is revealing regarding wellness needs.

LOVE

In early spring and again during January Venus, the celestial love goddess, blows kisses your way. Earth signs are involved so strolling outdoors, in a place of natural beauty, would provide the perfect romantic backdrop. The Full Moon eclipse on July 5 is in your birth sign. A revelation concerning a love bond is likely near then.

SPIRITUALITY

Your 9th house of higher consciousness and spiritual awareness promises insights during August and September and again near the Full Moon on February 27. Stones to heighten spiritual awareness include jet (for luck, protection and longevity) and snowflake obsidian (avoiding disaster).

FINANCE

An intense transit involving both Saturn and Jupiter impacts your 2nd house of finances from late December through the end of winter. Financial options materialize then; ventures are very promising. Efforts you make throughout the year are rewarded near your birthday.

AQUARIUS

January 20–February 18

Spring 2020– Spring 2021 for those
born under the sign of the Water Bearer

Expressing the authentic self is the
Water Bearer's style. There is joy in
pursuing humanitarian projects aimed
at improving the world. For this free-
spirited and curious idealist exploring
many places while getting to know
about different people adds zest to life.
Financial security is important, but
mainly for the freedom it can bring.
Aquarians have charisma. Others tend
to confide their concerns and secrets to
the empathetic ear of this natural counselor who is a friend to many.

Dedicate the Vernal Equinox to a
prosperity ritual. The springtime begins
with Mercury in your 2nd house of
finances. Through April 10 your ideas
and conversations will revolve around
cash flow and earnings. Your energy
level is high and a competitive spirit
motivates you April through May 12 as
Mars transits your birth sign. Dedicate
May Eve to a blessing for peace. By
mid-May, Jupiter will be retrograde in
your 12th house. Release old regrets as
spring unfolds. The June 5 lunar eclipse
accents new friendships and upcoming
vacation plans. Your health sector is
highlighted by Mercury and the Sun by
late June. The June 21 solar eclipse at
the Summer Solstice favors attending a

healing circle. That is also an optimum
time to adopt dietary improvements.

During July Venus hovers in your
5th house of love and pleasure. A
romantic liaison or enjoyable hobbies
make this a happy cycle. Decorate
at Lammastide and offer a token of
appreciation to one whom you cherish. The Aquarius Full Moon on
August 3 allows you to shine; your
talents will be in evidence. The 2nd
and 3rd weeks of August bring an
emphasis on teamwork, as your 7th
house sets the pace. Cooperation and
participation pave the route to progress.
A mercurial quality affects your 8th
house August 22–September 5. A mystery is solved. Communication with
the spirit world is likely. Consider
attending a séance or medium-
ship session. A lucky Venus transit
brings opportunities for a close partner from September 6–October 2.
Offer a compliment and celebrate the
accomplishments of one whose life is
a part of your own. October brings a
need for flexibility at work. Travel and
schedule is changes can be involved as
Mercury will turn retrograde on your
midheaven. The Full Blue Moon on
Halloween shines in your 4th house of
home and heritage. Honor All Hallows
with a house blessing. Let vintage
designs inspire your costume choice.

The first three weeks of November
Venus is in your 9th house. Pursue travel
and study. You will be able to exchange
ideas with others and communicate effectively. Honor the inner child at the eclipse
on November 30. Expect a turning point
regarding a romantic interest. A troubled
young person might need encouragement

as November ends. December centers on your 11th house. The Yuletide season brings an interest in community service and humanitarian projects. The total solar eclipse on December 14 attracts you to new associates, group affiliations and long-range goals. At the Winter Solstice prepare a blessing for the future, perhaps tapping into a favorite Tarot card for inspiration. December 19 finds Jupiter beginning a year-long passage through your birth sign. The winter season brings widening perspectives and growth. On January 14 Uranus completes its retrograde. Clarity of direction intensifies and loose ends are tied up before your birthday. The Full Moon on January 28 illuminates the parameters of a close relationship. You will frequent crowded public places and highly publicized events as the month ends.

At Candlemas Venus enters Aquarius. Add glittery and bejeweled pillar candles to an artistically appointed altar. The theme is one of love and beauty. By the Aquarius New Moon on February 11 both financial gain and social interactions take a positive turn. Late February–March 3 a Mars square to your Sun accents family dynamics. Seek to resolve differences amicably. Household maintenance and repairs can be needed. Venus joins Neptune in your financial sector during the last weeks of winter. Juggling spirituality with economic considerations occupies your thoughts. Meditate and reflect upon values. The New Moon on March 13 favors making wise use of available funds. Play games or enjoy sports March 14–20 when refreshing Mars influence focuses on recreation.

HEALTH
Because the Moon rules your health sector environmental concerns such as temperature extremes will affect wellness. Making your surroundings comfortable is essential. The eclipse on June 21 dynamically affects your health. Address concerns during the summer. Jupiter, the celestial healer, enters your sign on December 19, indicating improved health during the winter.

LOVE
Venus sits in your 5th house of love April 4–August 6. This promises romantic interludes. Maintain the status quo regarding a love commitment while Venus is retrograde May 13–June 25. The November 30 eclipse brings an interesting new direction regarding love.

SPIRITUALITY
The Full Moon on April 7 in your 9th house of higher consciousness promises spiritual awakening during the spring. The second and third weeks of September tie Mercury to spirituality. Visiting a sacred site or reading inspirational literature can broaden spiritual insights. Your spirit stones include lapis lazuli (for healing and following a higher purpose) and moldavite (for happiness, extra terrestrial connections and expanded awareness.)

FINANCE
Saving and preparing is the theme regarding finances. Serious Saturn transits Aquarius March 22–July 1 and again from December 17 through the end of winter. Being patient and realistic will bring gradual financial stability.

PISCES
February 19–March 20
Spring 2020–Spring 2021 for those
born under the sign of the Fish

Subjective interpretation and duality characterize the mild mannered pair of bound Fish. Forever swimming through the changeable sea of life they pull in different directions. Using the imagination to reorient themselves and transcend the pain of everyday life is the quest. The outlook on life is dreamlike and so very sensitive.

At the Vernal Equinox, Mercury joins Neptune in your 1st house, a trend in force until April 10. Include poetry in a seasonal celebration. Your eloquent expression of ideas will create a favorable impression. Make applications and requests. During mid to late April financial considerations are a focus. The Sun and other transits activate your money sector. Consider new developments linked to your source of income. May 1–12 a strong 3rd house emphasis points to involvement with neighborhood activities. Surprise deserving neighbors on May Day with pretty baskets or bouquets.

Mars is in your sign May 13–June 27, bringing an energy surge. Much can be accomplished. Enjoy dance and water sports. The June 21 eclipse is all about love and leisure. Present a potpourri of fragrant herbs and oils made at a seasonal celebration to someone you care for. During July retrograde Mercury sparks creative ideas. Consider enrolling in an arts and crafts class or try creative writing. Lammastide brings an optimum time to attend the theater, opera and other cultural events. August 7–September 10 Venus brightens your 5th house of love. Nurture a romance. Plan events to share with one whom you would woo. A shared dream or intuitive perception at the Full Moon in Pisces on September 2 deepens the love bond.

During September Jupiter and Saturn turn direct in your 11th house of personal wishes and future plans. Focus on where you would like to be in years to come. At the Autumnal Equinox on September 22, assemble a vision board collage illustrating what you would like to manifest. The Full Moon on October 1 joins Mars in your 2nd house of cash flow. Budget carefully and patiently build a security base. Offer those who seek help encouragement instead of financial assistance. By All Hallows monetary matters are improving. Halloween's Full Moon affects your 9th house of philosophy. Don a costume honoring a favorite god or goddess. Hecate, Pluto, the Crone or the Tarot's Hermit are some possibilities.

November 1–20 brings comforting insights and messages from the spirit realm, as Venus moves through your 8th house of afterlife connections. On November 29 Neptune turns direct in Pisces, your 1st house, bringing insights into who you are and what your life means. The eclipse on November 30 accents domestic matters. A residential move could be considered.

December 1–14 brings a pleasant trine from Venus to your Sun. Seasonal decorations, art and music enable you to capture the essence of Yuletide. The Winter Solstice brings two cosmic heavyweights, Jupiter and Saturn, over the cusp of your 12th house. A quiet and contemplative mood prevails on the longest of nights. Dreams are meaningful. As December ends you will become aware of how important a positive mindset is. Finding peace within helps manifest a productive life.

January 1–6 Venus completes a transit in your career sector. Friendships with supportive coworkers help you to advance. Mars changes signs on January 7 and exits your money sector. Financial pressures ease as Candlemas nears. Celebrate. Speak of gratitude by the light of a snow white taper. A stellium of planets plus the Sun clusters in your sector of charity and sacrifice during mid-February. A volunteer position and other charitable endeavors would be rewarding. Enjoy wilderness areas and attune to natural beauty.

During March, Venus conjoins your Sun. Focus on new garments and self care while celebrating your birthday. The New Moon on March 13 reveals how others see you and brings hints about how to make the best first impression. Mutable signs are strong March 14–20. Winter ends with a flurry of multitasking. Time passes quickly with so much going on.

HEALTH

While Neptune is retrograde in your 1st house June 23–November 29 correct any questionable health habits. This is also a good time to study wellness factors. The Full Moon on January 28 affects your 6th house of health. There can be a turning point regarding reaching health goals then.

LOVE

Mercury transits your 5th house of love May 29–August 4. Communication facilitates happiness in romance. Travel with a loved one. The solar eclipse on June 21 and the Full Moon on December 29 bring important developments regarding true love.

SPIRITUALITY

April 4–August 6 Venus, ruler of your natal 8th house of spirituality, transits your sector of residence and heritage. Spiritual truths can be found in analyzing the spiritual inclinations of ancestors. Creating a meditation corner or altar in your home would encourage spiritual growth too. Stones which harmonize with your spirituality include larimar (Atlantis connections, peace and clarity) and celestite (angelic attunement, higher awareness.)

FINANCE

Eclipses on June 5 and December 14 create a stir in your 10th house of career, auguring shifts in your income and financial plans. Be flexible. Mars transits your 2nd house of earned income June 28–January 6, indicating much energy invested in meeting financial expectations. The monetary outlook brightens during the winter.

Sites of Awe

The White Well of Glastonbury

I'm excited to be here in Glastonbury, England, home of the Chalice Well—the sacred Red Well, which is because of the heavy iron content in the water, and White Well, which gets its hue from the limestone it passes through. The red is associated with the Goddess and the white is associated with the God. I have been told several times this week that the White Well was closed because of work going on in the street, but I'm obviously going to go anyway, with fingers crossed!

As I walk down High Street, and turn right at the end, I'm hoping that the well's temple will be open today. The weather is beautiful and I am secretly thinking that we have a good sign here.

Traveling down Chikwell Street, I don't see any sign of it being closed, but won't be able to see fully until I get a bit closer. I'm excited and a bit anxious.

Turning onto Wellhouse Lane, I don't see any sign of workmen in the street. Okay, I can see the door from here and it is open!

On the left side of the road is a woman (probably a local resident), who is at the runoff faucet of the Red Well. I can see how the sidewalk has been stained red from the iron in the water. She has some empty jugs that she is filling. The Glastonbury residents know you can get water from the faucets in the street that route excess well water into the town's drain system.

On the right side of the street is the faucet for the excess White Well water. Next to it is a plant growing out of the stone wall where people have tied clooties. So many wishes, so many blessings. I did not think to bring a ribbon with me. So, tearing off a strip of cloth from the bottom

of my shirt, I tie it on while thinking of good health for those I love.

The sign at the door shows "no photos." There is an open stylized, green iron gate at the front door of the temple. It is dark inside. A man sits by the door, collecting offerings probably to support the Chalice Well Trust, and thereby the maintenance of this temple building. He is selling candles and incense for use inside. After placing something in the basket, I walk inside. I am choked up in awe of the atmosphere. Heavy with incense and thick with energy (best felt with your eyes closed).

The whispers of visitors seem almost drowned out by the silence of the space—only allowing the sound of moving water to come through. Silence—for what seemed like forever. This place is eternal. Time stops still here and everyone knows it. Most people are silent—out of respect, in awe or just because they have no choice and cannot speak.

There is what seems to be a large stone "vat-like" structure in the center of the room. It is filled with water and in some places, it seems to overflow onto the stone floor—which has gullies carved into it in order to move the excess water out of the walking space. This does little good as most of the floor is anywhere from wet to two inches deep with water.

As I walk up to this basin, which seems bottomless (but this is only an energetic illusion, as it is probably only three feet deep), I find myself almost instinctively reaching for the back of my neck to unfasten my neck chain. It holds about six charms. I'm drawn to hold the jewelry in my hands and to place my hands into the water. A feeling of cleanliness and energy transference happens as I stand still and allow my eyes to adjust to the dark, I can make out three areas that have been set up as shrines—one to my immediate left and one to the far right, almost behind the basin. As I walk around to the right of the basin, I can see a Maypole, covered in ribbons, laying on the floor. I was told to look for this. It is the Glastonbury Maypole, danced last week by the residents of the town. Now, the water on the floor is getting deeper as I approach what appears to be a Horned God shrine. I see a set of horns, images of the Horned God, candles, incense and many other offerings that are best not spoke of in this story. It would seem to almost break the

spell of power that enshrouds this shrine. I am overwhelmed. As far as Western European Pagan practices go, I have not seen this much energy emanating from a shrine in decades. It is metaphysically a very impressive site. I will later learn that this altar is set up to honor the King of the World of Faerie.

I'll spend some time here contemplating the God within, the horns, the stang, the power, the Light…

Moving back across the room, I see a couple of people talking outside the door. As they look inside, their voices immediately soften and their eyes widen. The energy from this room is flowing out to the street.

Here in the southeast corner of the room is an area dedicated to Brigid, the Great Mother. Branches hang overhead with clooties tied everywhere—hundreds of bright colors shine in the darkness. A large painting of the Great Mother is lit by tea lights. There are two benches flanking this alcove where I am able to sit and meditate on the outpouring of love, nurturing, creativity and power that "shines" here.

No more can be said. This temple needs to be experienced to understand. My words are just not conveying what I am sensing here. The best I can do is explain what I see and hear. But the White Well is best experienced with magic senses—closed eyes begin the process.

Lastly, in the southwest of the building is a small area marked with more offerings and candles. These appear to be acknowledging the source of the water itself, but I will later learn that this altar is set to honor Our Lady of Avalon.

Before I leave, I see a woman undress and wrap herself in a towel; and now, climbing into the basin—for healing, for a blessing, or just for pleasure? I won't ask. Solemnness, sanctity and the sacred command silence. No conversation that is not completely necessary should take place here.

The shrines are carefully set and cared for by the keepers of the spring. Further research will inform me that in order to keep the shrines clear and set as they were intended, the many offerings left at the shrines are respectfully moved to the seasonal altar. The seasonal altar changes every six weeks to reflect the changes of nature throughout the year, and offerings from the natural world are welcome.

My visit here is coming to an end. I don't know if I have been here fifteen minutes or two hours. Truly, being here in this shrine of the White Well is like entering Faerie.

This experience has changed me, morphed me, into a more sensitive and respectful magician and Witch. I will always honor and never forget my visit to Glastonbury's White Well.

—ARMAND TABER

Reviews

Weave the Liminal: Living Modern
Traditional Witchcraft
Laura Tempest Zakroff
Llewellyn Publications
ISBN-13: 978-0738756103

LIKE ANY declaration of self, to identify as a witch brings more questions
than answers. Who and what should be
considered genuinely helpful? What
does genuine or helpful even mean?
Do certain paths, teachers, or groups
improve or validate your practice more
than others? Does a fear of not being
or knowing enough affect how you
practice or determine if you pursue a
practice at all?

Laura's Aquarian approach frames
and addresses these questions and so
many more you didn't know to you
wanted to answers to. She helps YOU
decide what is best for you. Her writing
is a fun and easy conversation that leaves
you feeling renewed and ready for more,
like choosing gods – or not, or pursuing
some previously obscure witchy interest
that popped from the pages.

Laura's traveling workshops puts
her face-to-face with witches of every
age in all corners of the country. This
book is the map and compass to the
modern witch world. It will speak to
you, about you, and help you accept
your doubts and be kind to yourself
while seeking your way.

The Orphic Hymns: A New Translation
for the Occult Practitioner
Patrick Dunn
Llewellyn Publications
ISBN-13: 978-0738753447

THE HYMNS attributed to the mythical being Orpheus (and specifically, the
mystery cults who honored his name)
are some of the most beautiful examples
of ancient Pagan devotional poetry in
existence. Utilized by mystical seekers
for millennia, these beautiful paeans are
perfect for augmenting one's personal
spiritual work, while simultaneously
connecting it to a rich lineage of ancient
ritual songs and adorations.

Occultist, translator, and literature
professor Patrick Dunn thus had
his work cut out for him in adapting
these venerable verses for the modern
reader, but rest assured he does not
disappoint. His handling of the Hymns
is both fresh and reverential. They
can even be quite playful at times
without diminishing from the power
and gravitas of the original Hellenic
stanzas. Not fearing comparison, Dunn
has even included Thomas Taylor's
1792 translations of the texts for those
wishing to see what he was working
with from the English side of things.

The book has a beautiful side-by-
side, Classical Greek vs. English format
reminiscent of a Loeb Library codex

or some of the more recent Joseph H. Peterson books. Thus, those with a better knowledge of ancient languages can compare and contrast participles and contextual hints, while making use of the original text for further inspiration. An extensive concordance and glossary is an added bonus the reader will quickly appreciate when some of the lesser-known Greek names appear mid-line. Ultimately, the coolest edition of the Hymns any occultist could possibly want.

Transformative Witchcraft:
The Greater Mysteries
By Jason Mankey
Llewellyn Publications
ISBN-13: 978-0738757971

JASON MANKEY HAS a well-deserved reputation in the magical community for being a thoughtful and compassionate teacher and Witch. This obvious love and care for the numinous thread which connects us all flows through his writing with ease and a palpable warmth, and is a subtle joy to experience.

The title of his recent foray might feel somewhat vague and misleading (I mean, what Witchcraft isn't transformative, really?), especially since the bulk of the book feels to be an examination of rather traditional and in many cases, Wiccan-specific practices. However, Mankey is rather adept at parsing some tricky philosophical concepts in a way that is both erudite and engaging.

The beauty of this book has to do with its ability to impart a great deal of theory and context into the otherwise silent portions of the Wiccan corpus. In fact, as one reads the book, the more it feels

like it should be a required appendix to the classic works of modern initiatory Witchcraft—Gardner, Buckland, Valiente, the Farrars, et al. It expands and expounds without muddying or garbling anything, showing the richness and subtlety contained within Wiccan rituals and beyond. Well-crafted and definitely recommended.

Secrets of Solomon: A Witch's
Handbook from the Trial Records of
the Venetian Inquisition
by Joseph H. Peterson (translator)
CreateSpace Independent Publishing Platform
ISBN-13: 978-1720387053

IMAGINE IF YOU had the ability to get your hands on a Witch's book of shadows from four centuries ago and could compare its Latin spell verses and instructions with a side-by-side English translation. Well, wait no more.

Joseph Peterson has returned with another offering to the fascinating history of magic and occultism with this utter gem of a historical manuscript, painstakingly translating a practicing Witch's handbook confiscated by the Venetian Inquisition. Publishing its secrets for all in this unassuming and inexpensive book, his wonderful translation expands and deepens the lore of the grimoires, showing a snapshot between the earliest editions of the Grimoirium Verum and the later Goetia or Lesser Key of King Solomon, with spirit lists both familiar and alien to our modern eyes. At the same time, elements of folk traditions and superstitions pop up in the ritual directions in a way not unsimilar to older manuscripts such as the Hygromanteia, and even some corollaries to the Leyden Papyrus and other Graeco-Egyptian spells of the late Classical world can be found.

This recently-revealed treasure trove from Northern Italy is a magnificent snapshot into the world of a late-Renaissance occultist, and shows very clearly where Hermetic, Cunning Folk, and Luciferian strains of thought intersected and influenced each other in the mystical world of our early modern ancestors. Top marks!

The Witch's Book of Mysteries
By Devin Hunter
Llewellyn Publications
ISBN-13: 978-0738756561

THIS THIRD BOOK in a series focusing on expanding one's Witchcraft practice contains a surprisingly rich and fertile landscape within its slender slipcase. Hunter weaves personal tales of spirit contact and the struggles of religious freedom in his past with a highly clever yet intuitive style of ritual working, one which Traditional Witches, Wiccans and even Chaotes can easily get behind. Casual yet dense, his style is rather engaging without feeling as if you're being lectured.

The exercises really take key focus here, as the author is all about visualizations to aid in spellcasting, and many of the shall we say "classic" components are given a fresh perspective with plenty of wiggle-room for improvisation. There are also a few rather clever sigil techniques thrown in for good measure, which always tickle this reviewer's fancy

Hunter's energy-work exercises are great warm-ups to the larger, more complicated rituals and rites, though highly effective even when paired with simpler invocations, and his hands-on approach to just about everything is always a relief in a world so replete with "internet scholars" and other such pitfalls of the modern age.

The Alchemical Visions Tarot
By Arthur Taussig Phd.
Weiser Books
ISBN-13: 978-1578636419

A WORLD-RENOWNED artist, physicist, and fingerstyle guitarist whose works have been showcased in galleries around the globe, Arthur Taussig has decided to take the plunge into the rich polyverse of Tarot, with some stunning results.

Mixing decades of scientific inspiration with an artistic vision dripping with visceral beauty, Taussig weaves and wends the more classic Kabbalistic philosophies and Jungian psychology with a deeply immersive, somewhat surrealist vision of the Tarot. Combining mostly monochrome, greyscale shading with vibrant splashes of color and texture, he accents key symbols within each card in a way that leaps out at the querent, playing with eye and perspective in an emotional dance of wisdom and fervor. The images seem to emanate from the cards in ways that makes one think their fingers could find physical structures within the otherwise flat pictures. The accompanying book is a gem all its own, with well-researched and highly illuminating explanations of the curious figures and icons contained within each card.

A testament to the creative potency within archetypal images, the Alchemical Visions Tarot is a breathtaking tour through universal space both external and internal.

The Mirror of Magic: A History of Magic in the Western World
Kurt Seligman
Inner Traditions
ISBN-13: 978-1620557907

THIS 1948 classic is a glorious synopsis of Western occult history, prepared by one of the most well-known Swiss Surrealist painters of his time. Though primarily known for his artwork, painter and engraver Kurt Seligman was also a practicing occultist and historian with a rather impressive mystical, antiquarian library. This is of course brought to the forefront in his Mirror of Magic, as he combs his personal stacks to bring the reader oodles of intriguing historical tidbits found nearly nowhere else around.

Those of us who have been in the game a while will be happy to see Seligman's synopsis containing so many of the names and profiles of brilliant and influential occult minds now sadly missing from modern occult discourse. Names like Albertus Magnus, Pico della Mirandola, Roger Bacon, Iamblichus and our perpetual friend Agrippa.

The sheer number of classic illustrations and engravings is nearly worth the cover price alone, and Seligman does not merely show without telling. His descriptions and analyses of alchemical symbolism and mystical art trends are both inciteful and clever. Seligman's book on a whole is a gem

of historical magic, as beguiling now as it must have been when it was released 70 years ago.

Encounters with Nature Spirits: Co-creating with the Elemental Kingdom
R. Ogilvie Crombie
Findhorn Press
ISBN-13: 978-1620558379

IMAGINE YOUR favorite, charming, Scottish great-uncle was also a wizard who enjoyed talking to nature spirits. One day, after he passed, you found his diary and realized that not only was it brimming with fascinating records of his spirit contacts and conversations, but it could be easily published as the world's most faun-friendly memoir. The above is a legitimate approximation of what it feels like to read R. Ogilvie Crombie's Encounters with Nature Spirits.

Crombie, a self-taught historian and esotericist, shares his many experiences with fauns, land spirits, elementals, and even encounters with the Great God Pan himself. Eventually his rendezvous with the forest-dwelling, multi-dimensional folk would bring him to the Findhorn Community. Findhorn is a combination Ecovillage, New Age Retreat Center and preserve in Northern Scotland on the Moray coast, where 'Roc' would continue his curious meetings with denizens of the Greenwood realms.

Bringing forth a positive message of change and cooperation with the spirits of the elemental kingdoms and the ecology of Mother Earth herself, Encounters with Nature Spirits is a feel-good memoir ideal for a quiet read at home before the fire, or deep in the middle of the woods.

From a Witch's Mailbox

The Past and the Future

You published a very lovely book on Tarot a couple of years ago. Can you tell a little of its history and where I can get the deck?—Submitted by Jen O'Brien

It was great fun putting together Paul Huson's Dame Fortune's Wheel Tarot: A Pictorial Key. *The deck was based on Paul's own research surrounding the Parisian fortune teller, Jean-Baptiste (known also as Etteilla). It is his descriptions that are brought to life in the deck that the book details. The artwork is original to Paul. There is a charm to the imagery that is used and Paul's rendition of each is brilliant. We presented each card without adjustment when publishing* Dame Fortune's Wheel Tarot. *His deck can be purchased at https://www.amazon.com/Fortunes-Wheel-Tarot-English-Spanish/dp/0738715298. Happy divining to you!*

A ceremonious Witch

What is the relationship between Wicca and Ceremonial Magic?—Submitted by Darrel Johnson

The relationship between Ceremonial Magic and Wicca has been a long and deep one. How they have affected each other is complex and in some measure not completely documented. The Ceremonial and Grimoire traditions in Europe run deep. These traditions were not confined to "Pagans" rather many Christians and Jews practiced, as well as the cunning folk of the heath. Many a cunning man/woman used the techniques found in grimoires. Many of the older pantheons of the Middle East and Europe were adapted to Ceremonial practices. Disentangling them would be difficult. "Modern" Wicca certainly borrowed from older Ceremonial traditions for their liturgy. An informed Witch should have a rudimentary understanding of grimoire magic for at the very least history's sake.

Is it familiar

Is having a familiar really a thing in modern Witchcraft?—Submitted by Tom Vitkus

The short answer is yes, familiars are a real thing in modern Wicca. While most Witches are acquainted with the term, the definition of what a familiar is can vary. In classical texts and folklore, there are two types of familiars. The first is a spirit familiar. In this case the familiar is a helper spirit utilized to accomplish magical tasks. They are often magically fabricated energy that is given a lifespan and purpose by the Witch creating them. Another term for this kind of familiar is a "fetch." The second type of familiar is an animal who lives with the Witch. The spirit of these animals help protect the Witch, as well as aid in magical operations. Care must be taken when working with familiars, whichever the variety that you chose to work with. A good amount of thought and divination should precede working with them. In the case of a living animal, great care should be taken not to psychically harm the animal.

It's all in the stars

How much do I need to consider placement of the planets when planning my magical work?—Submitted by Emma Forge

In any magical task knowing all of the influences that may hinder or help your work can only be a good thing. The natural tides can greatly boost your endeavors. For instance, if monetary gain is an objective in your working, you certainly want to ensure that the Moon is waxing, that Venus is well aspected and that Mercury is not retrograde. How detailed you get is wholly a matter of your preferences and your knowledge base. There are many excellent books of Astrology that will help in building a knowledge base. A good start might be Practical Astrology for Witches and Pagans *by Ivo Dominguez.*

Which way is Norse

I absolutely love Norse mythology and feel incredibly drawn to the Norse Gods. Do I have to be of Nordic ancestry to participate in Nordic groups?—Submitted by Angela Crettela

At The Witches' Almanac, we truly believe that pursuing a practice should be based on what feels right to your soul, not your ancestral ethnicity. Restricting anyone's practice because of their ethnic background is anathema to the Divine, which transcends such silliness. You will need to exercise a bit of discre-tion in your endeavor to associate with those who have the same interest. There are a number of organizations that unfortunately espouse an "ethnic purity" for their members. You should take time to research a group that you are interested in. Generally those that label themselves as Asatru do not discriminate based on ethnic background. A bit of some good advice from the Havamal: "The watchful guest, when he arrives for a meal, should keep his mouth shut, listening with his ears and watching with his eyes..."

Let us hear from you, too

We love to hear from our readers. Letters should be sent with the writer's name (or just first name or initials), address, daytime phone number and e-mail address, if available. Published material may be edited for clarity or length. All letters and e-mails will become the property of The Witches' Almanac Ltd. *and will not be returned. We regret that due to the volume of correspondence we cannot reply to all communications.*

The Witches' Almanac, Ltd.
P.O. Box 1292
Newport, RI 02840-9998
info@TheWitchesAlmanac.com
www.TheWitchesAlmanac.com

192

The products and services offered above are paid advertisements.

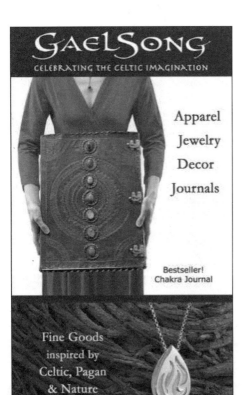

≈ MARKETPLACE ≈

The products and services offered above are paid advertisements.

ᔉMARKETPLACE ᔈ

www.AzureGreen.net Jewelry, Amulets, Incense, Oils, Herbs, Candles, Statuary, Gemstones, Ritual Items. Wholesale inquiries welcome.

The Crystal Fox 311 Main Street, Laurel, MD 20707 USA. The largest new age/metaphysical gift shop in the mid-Atlantic region. Monday-Saturday 10am-9pm Sunday 11am-7pm. **(301) 317-1980**, sterling@thecrystalfox.com, www.thecrystalfox.com

The Great Witch from The Seven Sisters of Salem Tarot cards, psychic, Spiritual Balance and Love Spells. Call Kathleena (773) 677 9247

Mardukite Truth Seeker Press Legendary books and tomes of magick by Joshua Free. Necronomicon Anunnaki Bible, Sorcerer's Handbook, Arcanum, Book of Pheryllt & more! mardukite.com NecroGate.com

Starwind Gifts Starwind Gifts New Orleans, LA. Incense, candles, crystals, jewelry, cards, tarot & oracles, herbs, handmade soap, & services. (504) 595-9627 www.StarwindGifts.com

Twisted Broomstick Custom spell kits for all desires. Use code *WITCHSHIP* for free shipping on all orders over $50. www.TwistedBroomstick.com

The products and services offered above are paid advertisements.

TO: The Witches' Almanac
P.O. Box 1292, Newport, RI 02840-9998

www.TheWitchesAlmanac.com

Name_____

Address_____

City_____ State_____ Zip_____

E-mail_____

WITCHCRAFT being by nature one of the secretive arts, it may not be as easy to find us next year. If you'd like to make sure we know where you are, why don't you send us your name and address? You will certainly hear from us.

Atramentous Press

Revealing the inner secrets of traditional practices and occult philosophies

---

The Witches' Almanac is now the exclusive distributor of
Atramentous Press publications in America:

The Book of Q'ab iTz
by David Herrerias

The Witching-Other: Explorations and Meditations on the Existential Witch
by Peter Hamilton-Giles

Welsh Witches: Narratives of Witchcraft and Magic From 16th- And 17th-Century Wales
by Richard Suggett with foreword by Ronald Hutton

Standing at the Crossroads: Dialectics of the Witching-Other
by Peter Hamilton-Giles with Illustrations by Carolyn Hamilton-Giles

Atramentous Press has been initiated as a platform for exploring the mystical and philosophical approaches found in and amongst traditional practices. Encompassing the world of western occultism from Traditional Witchcraft to Ceremonial Magic, from indigenous folkloric practices. It is our aim to open up the debate about how meaning, history, knowledge, magic, superstition, and folklore are understood and applied in various cultural religious practice-based settings. It is by opening up the debate we discover how the meaning, history, knowledge, magic, superstition, and folklore are understood and applied in various cultural religious practice based settings

For information visit TheWitchesAlmanac.com/Atramentous/

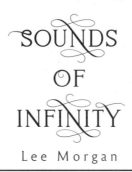

SOUNDS
OF
INFINITY

Lee Morgan

The Witches' Almanac presents:

• Faeries explored from a global perspective
• A poetic understanding and exploration of Faery
• A modern grimoire of Faery workings

We are pleased to welcome Lee Morgan to our imprint. His latest tome, *Sounds of Infinity*, treats us to a comprehensive look at the world of Faery exploring geographical understanding, poetic understanding, and finally presents a very a workable grimoire. This book is about something so hidden it can never be the object of a direct gaze. For this reason this book aims to watch the faerie obliquely, off to the side a little, via a mixture of primary source study, ritual and art.

272 pages — $24.95

For further information visit TheWitchesAlmanac.com/SoundsofInfinity

THE MAGIC
OF HERBS

David Conway

The Witches' Almanac presents:

• Revised and updated with current understandings
• Explanations of herbal decotions, tinctures and poultices
• Foreword by Colin Wilson

David Conway has revised and updated his seminal work, *The Magic of Herbs*. David was reared in a rural setting hecame to know about healing arts through practical application. In this update of *The Magic of Herbs*, he shares the knowledge of herbs he gained in his early training in the hills of the Welsh countryside, as well as new emerging information. David studied with a master herbalist near his boyhood home.

200 pages — $24.95

For further information visit TheWitchesmanac.com/MagicOfHerbs

MAGIC

An Occult Primer

David Conway

Aradia
Gospel of the Witches
Charles Godfrey Leland

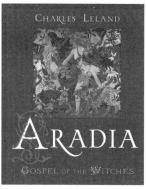

ARADIA IS THE FIRST work in English in which witchcraft is portrayed as an underground old religion, surviving in secret from ancient Pagan times.

- Used as a core text by many modern Neo-Pagans.
- Foundation material containing traditional witchcraft practices
- This special edition features appreciations by such authors as Paul Huson, Raven Grimassi, Judika Illes, Michael Howard, Christopher Penczak, Myth Woodling, Christina Oakley Harrington, Patricia Della-Piana, Jimahl di Fiosa and Donald Weiser. A beautiful and compelling work, this edition is an up to date format, while keeping the text unchanged. 172 pages $16.95

The ABC of Magic Charms
Elizabeth Pepper

Mankind has sought protection from mysterious forces beyond mortal control. Humans have sought the help of animal, mineral, vegetable. The enlarged edition of *Magic Charms from A to Z*, guides us in calling on these forces. $12.95

The Little Book of Magical Creatures
Elizabeth Pepper and Barbara Stacy

AN UPDATE of the classic *Magical Creatures*, featuring Animals Tame, Animals Wild, Animals Fabulous—plus an added section of enchanting animal myths from other times, other places. *A must for all animal lovers.* $12.95

The Witchcraft of Dame Darrel of York
Charles Godfrey Leland, Introduction by Robert Mathiesen

A beautifully reproduced facsimile of the illuminated manuscript shedding light on the basis for a modern practice. A treasured by those practicing Pagans, as well as scholars.   Standard Hardcover $65.00 or Exclusive full leather bound, numbered and slipcased edition $145.00

DAME FORTUNE'S WHEEL TAROT: A PICTORIAL KEY
Paul Huson

Based upon Paul Huson's research in *Mystical Origins of the Tarot, Dame Fortune's Wheel Tarot* illustrates for the first time the earliest, traditional Tarot card interpretations as collected in the 1700s by Jean-Baptiste Alliette. In addition to detailed descriptions, full color reproductions of Huson's original designs for all 79 cards.

WITCHES ALL

A Treasury from past editions, is a collection from *The Witches' Almanac* publications of the past. Arranged by topics, the book, like the popular almanacs, is thought provoking and often spurs the reader on to a tangent leading to even greater discovery. It's perfect for study or casual reading,

GREEK GODS IN LOVE

Barbara Stacy casts a marvelously original eye on the beloved stories of Greek deities, replete with amorous oddities and escapades. We relish these tales in all their splendor and antic humor, and offer an inspired storyteller's fresh version of the old, old mythical magic.

MAGIC CHARMS FROM A TO Z

A treasury of amulets, talismans, fetishes and other lucky objects compiled by the staff of *The Witches' Almanac*. An invaluable guide for all who respond to the call of mystery and enchantment.

LOVE CHARMS

Love has many forms, many aspects. Ceremonies performed in witchcraft celebrate the joy and the blessings of love. Here is a collection of love charms to use now and ever after.

MAGICAL CREATURES

Mystic tradition grants pride of place to many members of the animal kingdom. Some share our life. Others live wild and free. Still others never lived at all, springing instead from the remarkable power of human imagination.

ANCIENT ROMAN HOLIDAYS

The glory that was Rome awaits you in Barbara Stacy's classic presentation of a festive year in Pagan times. Here are the gods and goddesses as the Romans conceived them, accompanied by the annual rites performed in their worship. Scholarly, lighthearted – a rare combination.

CELTIC TREE MAGIC

Robert Graves in *The White Goddess* writes of the significance of trees in the old Celtic lore. *Celtic Tree Magic* is an investigation of the sacred trees in the remarkable Beth-Luis-Nion alphabet and their role in folklore, poetry and mysticism.

MOON LORE

As both the largest and the brightest object in the night sky, and the only one to appear in phases, the Moon has been a rich source of myth for as long as there have been mythmakers.

MAGIC SPELLS
AND INCANTATIONS

Words have magic power. Their sound, spoken or sung, has ever been a part of mystic ritual. From ancient Egypt to the present, those who practice the art of enchantment have drawn inspiration from a treasury of thoughts and themes passed down through the ages.

LOVE FEASTS

Creating meals to share with the one you love can be a sacred ceremony in itself. With the Witch in mind, culinary adept Christine Fox offers magical menus and recipes for every month in the year.

RANDOM RECOLLECTIONS
II, III, IV

Pages culled from the original (no longer available) issues of *The Witches' Almanac*, published annually throughout the 1970s, are now available in a series of tasteful booklets. A treasure for those who missed us the first time around, keepsakes for those who remember.

Order Form

Each timeless edition of *The Witches' Almanac* is unique.
Limited numbers of previous years' editions are available.

Item	Price	Qty.	Total
2020-2021 The Witches' Almanac – Stones: The Foundation of Earth	$12.95		
2019-2020 The Witches' Almanac – Animals: Friends & Familiars	$12.95		
2018-2019 The Witches' Almanac – The Magic of Plants	$12.95		
2017-2018 The Witches' Almanac – Water: Our Primal Source	$12.95		
2016-2017 The Witches' Almanac – Air: the Breath of Life	$12.95		
2015-2016 The Witches' Almanac – Fire:, the Transformer	$12.95		
2014-2015 The Witches' Almanac – Mystic Earth	$12.95		
2013-2014 The Witches' Almanac – Wisdom of the Moon	$11.95		
2012-2013 The Witches' Almanac – Radiance of the Sun	$11.95		
2011-2012 The Witches' Almanac – Stones, Powers of Earth	$11.95		
2010-2011 The Witches' Almanac – Animals Great & Small	$11.95		
2009-2010 The Witches' Almanac – Plants & Healing Herbs	$11.95		
2008-2009 The Witches' Almanac – Divination & Prophecy	$10.95		
2007-2008 The Witches' Almanac – The Element of Water	$9.95		
2003, 2004, 2005, 2006 issues of The Witches' Almanac	$8.95		
1999, 2000, 2001, 2002 issues of The Witches' Almanac	$7.95		
1995, 1996, 1997, 1998 issues of The Witches' Almanac	$6.95		
1993, 1994 issues of The Witches' Almanac	$5.95		
SALE: Bundle I—8 Almanac back issues (1991, 1993–1999) with free book bag	$ 50.00		
Bundle II— 10 Almanac back issues (2000–2009) with free book bag	$65.00		
Bundle III— 10 Almanac back issues (2010–2019) with free book bag	$100.00		
Bundle IV—28 Almanac back issues (1991, 1993–2019) with free book bag	$195.00		
Dame Fortune's Wheel Tarot: A Pictorial Key	$19.95		
Magic: An Occult Primer	$24.95		
The Witches' Almanac Coloring Book	$12.00		
The Witchcraft of Dame Darrel of York, clothbound, signed and numbered, in slip case	$85.00		
The Witchcraft of Dame Darrel of York, leatherbound, signed and numbered, in slip case	$145.00		
Aradia or The Gospel of the Witches	$16.95		
The Horned Shepherd	$16.95		
The ABC of Magic Charms	$12.95		
The Little Book of Magical Creatures	$12.95		
Greek Gods in Love	$15.95		
Witches All	$13.95		
Ancient Roman Holidays	$6.95		
Celtic Tree Magic	$7.95		
Love Charms	$6.95		
Love Feasts	$6.95		
Magic Charms from A to Z	$12.95		
Magical Creatures	$12.95		

Magic Spells and Incantations	$12.95		
Moon Lore	$7.95		
Random Recollections II, III or IV (circle your choices)	$3.95		
The Rede of the Wiccae – Hardcover	$49.95		
The Rede of the Wiccae – Softcover	$22.95		
Keepers of the Flame	$20.95		
Subtotal			
Tax *(7% sales tax for RI customers)*			
Shipping & Handling *(See shipping rates section)*			
TOTAL			

BRACELETS			
Item	**Price**	**QTY.**	**Total**
Agate, Green	$5.95		
Agate, Moss	$5.95		
Agate, Natural	$5.95		
Jade, White	$5.95		
Jasper, Picture	$5.95		
Jasper, Red	$5.95		
Quartz Crystal	$5.95		
Sodalite	$5.95		
Subtotal			
Tax (7% for RI Customers)			
Shipping and Handling			
Total			

MISCELLANY			
Item	**Price**	**QTY.**	**Total**
L-Sleeve T, Black	$15.00		
L-Sleeve T, Red	$15.00		
S-Sleeve T, Black/W	$15.00		
S-Sleeve T, Black/R	$15.00		
S-Sleeve T, Dk H/R	$15.00		
S-Sleeve T, Dk H/W	$15.00		
S-Sleeve T, Red/B	$15.00		
S-Sleeve T, Ash/R	$15.00		
S-Sleeve T, Purple/W	$15.00		
Postcards – set of 12	$3.00		
Bookmarks – set of 12	$12.00		
Magnets – set of 3	$1.50		
Promo Pack	$7.00		
Subtotal			
Tax (7% for RI Customers)			
Shipping and Handling			
Total			

MISCELLANY			
Item	**Price**	**QTY.**	**Total**
Pouch	$3.95		
Natural/Black Book Bag	$17.95		
Red/Black Book Bag	$17.95		
Hooded Sweatshirt, Blk	$30.00		
Hooded Sweatshirt, Red	$30.00		

SHIPPING & HANDLING CHARGES

BOOKS: One book, add $5.95. Each additional book add $1.50.

POUCH: One pouch, $3.95. Each additional pouch add $1.50.

BOOKBAGS: $5.95 per bookbag. **BRACELETS:** $3.95 per bracelet.

Send a check or money order payable in U. S. funds or credit card details to:

The Witches' Almanac, Ltd., PO Box 1292, Newport, RI 02840-9998

(401) 847-3388 (phone) • (888) 897-3388 (fax)
Email: info@TheWitchesAlmanac.com • www.TheWitchesAlmanac.com